Winning Arguments

ALSO BY STANLEY FISH

Winning Arguments

What Works and Doesn't Work in Politics, the Bedroom, the Courtroom, and the Classroom

STANLEY FISH

HARPER

NEW YORK · LONDON · TORONTO · SYDNEY

A hardcover edition of this book was published in 2016 by Harper, an imprint of HarperCollins Publishers.

WINNING ARGUMENTS. Copyright © 2016 by Stanley Fish. All rights reserved. Printed in the United States of America. No part of this book may be used or reproduced in any manner whatsoever without written permission except in the case of brief quotations embodied in critical articles and reviews. For information, address HarperCollins Publishers, 195 Broadway, New York, NY 10007.

HarperCollins books may be purchased for educational, business, or sales promotional use. For information, please e-mail the Special Markets Department at SPsales@harpercollins.com.

FIRST HARPER PAPERBACK EDITION PUBLISHED 2017.

Designed by Lucy Albanese

Library of Congress Cataloging-in-Publication Data has been applied for.

ISBN 978-0-06-222667-9 (pbk.)

17 18 19 20 21   OV/LSC   10 9 8 7 6 5 4 3 2 1

To the memory of Richard Rorty, 1931–2007.
"There is no such thing as non-discursive access to truth."

CONTENTS

◆――――――◆

INTRODUCTION, OR WHAT
THIS BOOK PROMISES TO DO

◆——————◆

THIS BOOK TRIES to do two things that might seem to pull against each other, but in the end I don't think they do.

The first thing this book tries to do is explain how argument works in different contexts. Say you're a politician, and you want to persuade people to vote for you. What kind of arguments can you make and what arguments might you do better to avoid? Or suppose you are—as almost everyone is—in a long-term domestic relationship fraught with tensions, some out in the open, others simmering just below the surface. Is there any way of making your case that doesn't increase the tensions rather than damping them down? Or say you find yourself in court. What arguments will a judge allow you to make and what arguments will be ruled inadmissible, not because they are "bad" arguments, but because the judicial system doesn't recognize them as appropriately legal? Or suppose you are a college teacher eager to advance in the profession by making arguments that will be compelling to your peers. There are any number of things you might say about the materials you are analyzing, but how do you know which of the things you might say will win you points in the game, and which will mark you as a nonserious player?

These are questions with answers, and you will find them in the pages that follow. But even as I go about supplying those answers, I am also engaged in another project, not quite parallel, but not unrelated either. I am making an argument about argument and its relationship to the human condition. Basically, argument is the medium we swim in, whether we want to or not. Argument, the clash of opposing views, is unavoidable because the state of agreement that would render argument unnecessary—a universal agreement brought about by facts so clear that no rational being could deny them—is not something we mortals will ever achieve. Each of us occupies a partial, time-bound perspective and none of us has access to the God's-eye view from which the "big picture" might be seen at a glance. Therefore any statement any of us makes is an argument because, as an assertion that proceeds from an angle, it can always be, and almost always will be, challenged by those whose vision is also angled, but differently so. Conflict, not agreement, is the default condition of mortality.

What this means is that knowledge and truth rather than presiding over the field of argument are what emerge in the course of argument; and because it is argument and not Reality with a capital R that produces them, truth and knowledge are always in the process of being renegotiated. There is no end, no stopping point, to this process and there is no end to—no resolution of—argument.

Many people do not wish to believe this. They believe in the possibility of identifying something that will neutralize argument, stop its vertigo, tame it—a common ground or an impersonal algorithm that will stand to the side of argument and supply a safe oasis of rest and consent. These dreamers emerge in every age, and offer a new (or apparently new) version of a very old project: let us, they say, refine and reform our language practices and develop a way of speaking and writing that has filtered out bias and prejudice in advance; then we will only be able to speak truth because the instrument we employ admits nothing else. Conflict will cease and argument can be retired or turned into a performance art.

To which I say: lots of luck, forget about it (but no one will) and learn to live with what we are and what we have. We are limited creatures who can only see through a glass darkly, and will never experience a face-to-face encounter with the Real; that encounter may await us in another life, but not in this one. In this one we look and see and talk and hope that by talking we can win others over to our side, which will always be a side, even when we proclaim it the full and complete truth. In short, we argue.

So repeat after me: argument is everywhere, argument is unavoidable, argument is interminable, argument is all we have.

LIVING IN A WORLD
OF ARGUMENT

◆————————◆

Words Make the World

IN A FAMOUS Monty Python sketch called "The Argument Clinic," a man played by Michael Palin enters an office and says to the receptionist, "I'd like to have an argument, please." What is odd about this request is that it doesn't specify what the argument is to be about. Any topic, it seems, will do, and as it turns out, no topic is put on the table, for Palin and his interlocutors (he is shunted from office to office) never proceed beyond arguing about what is and is not an argument. But of course that *is* a topic and, in the absence of some more substantive disagreement, it becomes substantive itself; the argument about argument fills the argumentative space and acquires a momentum of its own, and that momentum is uncontrollable.

The Palin character tries to control it and get a secure footing by putting a limit on the form argument can take. He objects that one of his argument partners (played by John Cleese) is not really arguing but just contradicting: "An argument," he insists, "is a connected series of statements intended to establish a proposition," while a contradiction "is just the automatic gainsaying of any statement the other person makes." The reply is brief and brilliant: "No it isn't." Or, in other (and more) words, "You say that contradiction can be cleanly distinguished from argument, but I refute your point—that is, argue against it—simply by denying it and thereby putting both of us in the position of having to give reasons; you now have to explain why contradiction has no place in the field of argument, and I have to explain why contradiction can be a move in the argument game, as I have just demonstrated it is; so *there*!" The amount of words I have had to expend in order to gloss "No it isn't" is testimony to the wonderful conciseness of the Cleese character's retort.

This sketch teaches (at least) three lessons: (1) You can't just engage in argument in the abstract. An abstract argument—an argument where there is nothing at stake and you are just practicing the form—is what the Palin character asks for, but before he knows it he is enmeshed in a very specific argument (about argument) and the cool distance he affects when announcing "I'd like to have an argument, please" gives way quickly to the exasperation that always attends the real thing. (2) You can neither avoid argument when it is offered to you nor extricate yourself from it on your terms. When the Palin character grows tired of the game and says, "I've had enough of this," his partner-in-agon replies, "No you haven't," and it begins all over again. (3) You cannot manage argument. The career of argument is always running ahead of the intentions and desires of those who engage in it; as an arguer you're always playing catch-up, trying to deal with the twists and turns you had not anticipated.

A fourth, more overarching, lesson follows from the first three. There are no general strategies for conducting an argument because the specific something arguments are always about will always be embedded in a social or institutional setting in relation to which some, but not all, strategies will be relevant and, at least potentially, effective. In the political arena, one tried-and-true strategy is to smear or "swift boat" your opponent, accusing him or her of all manner of crimes, lies, betrayals, indecencies, improprieties, and failures of judgment. But if you do that in an academic argument—an argument between two scholars about the interpretation of a poem or the correct account of a historical event—you might be rebuked and sent away because you will have flouted the decorum of the academic game. The ways of argument are context-specific, and while there are surely some general things to be said about argument, and an entire intellectual tradition called rhetoric dedicated to saying them, in the end the study of argument will be a study of the various contexts in which one encounters argument in its various forms.

One general thing that can properly be said about argument is that it is essentially the art of persuasion, the art of trying to move someone from an adherence to position A—which might be political, economic, domestic, aesthetic, military, theological, whatever—to an embracing of position B. Here is a very small example. An eleven-year-old boy wants to go to the mall with his friends. His mother says, "No." He asks, "Why," short for "What are your reasons?" She replies, "Because I say so." Is that a reason? Is she making an argument? We might think that the answer to both questions is no; she's just asserting her authority, putting her foot down. But that would be to make the mistake made by the Palin character when he declares that to contradict is not to argue. Argument is protean—ever changing, variable, mutable, kaleidoscopic, voracious—and almost anything can be its vehicle, swinging a big stick, putting on a badge, intoning a holy phrase, making the sign of the cross, wearing a uniform, speaking in a stentorian tone. In the venerable tradition that codifies and analyzes the making of arguments, the boy's mother is performing a standard move. It is called, not surprisingly, the "argument from authority" (*argumentum ab auctoritate*) and it is listed by Aristotle as one of his twenty-eight "common topics," the everyday strategies one might have recourse to in a situation of debate or dispute. As Aristotle explains in his *Rhetoric*, you reach for the argument from authority in order to link your view to a prestigious source such as "the Gods, or one's father, or one's teachers." You declare, I must be right because the Pope or the Supreme Court or Plato or Abraham Lincoln says what I say. (It is a nice point that Aristotle, after naming the argument from authority, became one.)

The argument from authority was given a television spot some years ago when the brokerage firm E. F. Hutton ran a series of famous ads in which one of the actors begins a sentence with these words: "My broker, E. F. Hutton, says . . ." Immediately all those within earshot stop whatever they were doing and lean toward the speaker in order to hear, and perhaps profit by, E. F. Hutton's advice. A voice-over intones the message: "When E. F. Hutton speaks, everyone listens." E. F. Hutton authorizes itself as an authority at the same moment its spokesman cites that authority (self-referentially) as an argument. The mother of the eleven-year-old boy does the same thing: she assumes the authority she then cites as a reason; the full version of "Because I say so" is "Because I'm your mother and I say so." In both cases authority is at once claimed and created by the rhetorical act of invoking it.

I tried that once and got my head handed to me. My six-year-old daughter, her mother, and I were sitting eating dinner. Conversation was difficult because my daughter was "interacting" (the reason for the quotation marks around the word will soon be obvious) with our two dachshunds, who were under the table. I said to her in that "I'm your father" voice, "Susan, don't play with the dachshunds." She showed me her hands in a classic "look, Pa, no hands" gesture, and said, "I'm not playing with the dachshunds." I regrouped and tried again: "Susan, don't kick the dachshunds." She pointed to the gentle motions of her feet and said, "I'm not kicking the dachshunds." Determined to come up with a formulation so general and inclusive that it would leave no room for further argument, I said in a tone of (premature) triumph, "Susan, don't do *anything* with the dachshunds." Not missing a beat, she replied, "You mean I don't have to feed them anymore?" (Score: six-year-old, 3; thirty-five-year-old college professor, 0.)

Two things were immediately clear. (1) This could have gone on forever: she would have been able to recontextualize any supposedly hard-and-fast statement I came up with in a way that altered its meaning and evaded its intended force. (2) My attempt to assert the authority of a father with the help of my adult rhetorical skills was a dismal flop. I am ashamed to say that I brought the matter to a close by slapping her (itself an argument, but a suspect one), an action that sealed her triumph rather than reversing it. I was showing myself to be both a bad father and a hapless debater. I neither exercised the supposedly natural authority of a parent nor created an authority by an artful use of words.

In the context of these examples, one might ask, is a rhetorically achieved authority inferior to the "real thing," to an authority established by an independent, nonrhetorical measure, an authority we might call "natural" as opposed to confected? Or are all authorities manufactured rather than found, which would mean that all authorities, even those that present themselves as undoubted and self-evident, are rhetorical constructions and therefore vulnerable to challenge, as I certainly was in the interaction with my daughter? That is a question we shall return to repeatedly—and let me tip my hand by saying that the second alternative is the correct one.

Although the argument from authority is always presented as being in need of no other support but itself—this is the way it is and there's nothing else to say—its force is a function of arguments already in place. You can't make an argument for authority unless the question of what is and is not an authority has been answered. So, as we have already seen, the invocation of an authority often goes hand in hand with its creation or at least its attempted creation. This is often what happens in the law, where the argument from authority is called precedent or stare decisis. Precedent is the practice of citing past decisions of courts in support of a present holding: judges say, we decide the case this way because it squares with what the Court of Appeals for the Seventh Circuit said in *Smith v. Jones* or *Black v. White*.

Precedents are described in the legal literature as either binding or persuasive. The truth is that they are binding *if* persuasive, if they have been successfully argued for. In response to the citing of a precedent, one can always dispute its relevance by saying that another case would be more on point, or dispute its status as a precedent by saying that it does not stand for the proposition you want to advance. Merely to call a prior case a precedent will not be decisive; it must be linked in a persuasive way with the issues thought to be in play in the present case. There has to be an argument to support the argument. And the effort might fail; the relevant audience, a judge or a court, may remain unpersuaded, just as the boy who is told he can't go to the mall may continue to press his case, my daughter may continue to play with the dogs, and the TV viewer may decide to stay with his current broker rather than come over to E. F. Hutton.

This is a key point: failure, at least as a possibility, is a condition of argument, for argument is, as Aristotle and everyone after him has said, the realm of the probable, the medium of exchange we engage in when the field of inquiry is structured by doubt and the absolute authority of God's word or a mode of perfect calculation is not available. (If it were available, doubt would soon be dispelled, and there would be no reason to argue.) In the absence of such an authority the response to doubt is to argue, to put forward theses and proofs in the hope the matter can be clarified to the satisfaction of at least a majority of those in the relevant audience.

And that of course does happen, but not in a final way. Argument could be final in its effect only if it were rooted in an objective ground that narrowed the area of doubt, present and future, to nothing. But since the theses and proofs argument brandishes are themselves disputable, the victory of any set of them and the establishing of consensus will only be temporary, will last only so long as the newly urged theses and proofs (or the same old ones repackaged) unsettle the consensus and put in place—again temporarily—a new one. In a world bereft of transcendence, argument cannot achieve certainty; it can only achieve persuasion (and may not do even that), a resolving of the issue that lasts only until a more powerful act of persuasion supplants it.

One might think that the cycle of arguments beating down and supplanting previous arguments might be broken by some independent yardstick—some yardstick outside the arena of argument—that gives us criteria for distinguishing the good arguments from the bad ones. But this would be a possibility only if such a yardstick could be uncontroversially identified. It is not that there are no such yardsticks—they are offered all the time—it's just that once offered they become objects of controversy themselves; they become fodder for the forensic wars they were supposed to put a stop to. Argument could produce certainty only if we lived in a world where a settled dispute stays settled because its resolution has been accomplished by a measure everyone accepts and accepts permanently. Then argument would be a matter of deduction from universally established principles; it would be a tool of those principles, a tool that could be discarded when it performed its merely instrumental task of serving something larger and more abiding than itself.

But we don't live in that world. We live in a world where God and Truth have receded, at least as active, perspicuous presences, and the form they take at any moment will be the result of a proposition successfully urged, of an argument: believe me, *this* is what God is like and what he wants, or, believe me, *this* is the truth of the matter. Rhetorically created authorities are all we have; absolute authority exists only in a heaven we may hope someday to see, but until that day we must make do with the epistemological resources available to us in our fallen condition; we must make do with argument. For all intents and purposes, and as far as we know or can know, we live in a world of argument. Indeed, arguments about the world come first, the world comes second.

The Desire for Another World

That conclusion has always been resisted by those who see in it the end of reasoned discourse and of the ability to say of something that it is right or wrong. If nothing, not even truth, can stand against the power of words, if someone skilled in speaking can, as Aristotle put it, make the worse appear the better, all is lost and we might as well throw up our hands and do whatever we like. It is in the context of such a fearsome prospect that rhetoric has gotten bad press and been stigmatized as the medium of charlatans, deceivers, propagandists, admen, all of whom take advantage of man's susceptibility to base and illegitimate appeals and perfect the art of leading hearers by the nose to conclusions that serve some special interest rather than the interests of society.

Francis Bacon, one of the founders of the scientific method, warned in the early seventeenth century that the project of apprehending "the true divisions of nature" (a nice definition of science's aim) is always being torpedoed by words that refuse to be confined to the modest task of mirroring a prior reality and instead offer themselves as a substitute for the facts they should be faithfully representing. Bacon believed that the power of language to lead men astray is one of the unhappy consequences of the Fall. The tendency of fallen creatures to love the words they produce more than the truth the words supposedly serve is an effect, he says, "of that venom which the Serpent infused . . . which makes the mind of man to swell."

No such theological speculations inform the best-known modern example of the antirhetorical stance, George Orwell's "Politics and the English Language" (1946). In this famous and influential essay, Orwell argues that the decay of political conditions—he cites the rise of fascism and communism—goes hand in hand with the decay of linguistic conditions: "the present political chaos is connected with the decay of language . . . the German, Russian and Italian languages have all deteriorated in the last ten or fifteen years as a result of dictatorship." If your language goes wrong, your politics will go wrong and vice versa. And what does it mean for language to go wrong? It means that language is guiding thought rather than the other way around: "the worst thing one can do with words is surrender to them," that is, allow them to define the shape of fact as opposed to allowing the shape of fact to dictate the choice of words.

The way to avoid this unhappy situation, Orwell counsels, is "to think wordlessly, and then, if you want to describe the thing you have been visualizing you . . . hunt around until you find the exact words that seem to fit it." Indeed, he adds, "it is better to put off using words as long as possible," and think instead "through pictures." But this advice makes sense only if the "thing" it is the job of words to match has a "wordless" reality to which we can have nonverbal access. Those who believe that we live in a rhetorical world will say that thinking wordlessly is something that can't be done because the objects of thought—natural phenomena, political policies, urban landscapes, historical periods—become available for our attention only when the system of differences that constitute a language makes it possible to point to them, a pointing that could not have been performed independently of that system. Historians talk easily about things like the Middle Ages, the Renaissance, the Romantic period, and the Modern period. But the men and women who lived during those times (which were not "times" to them, just the days of their lives) did not identify themselves as Medieval or Renaissance or Modern.

Those categories—and the "realities" they name—emerged only after scholars had carved history up at the joints, joints that were not there before the carving up; they are produced by words, not by brute fact.

Even when we think through pictures as Orwell advises, what we picture will have assumed its shape as a consequence of the linguistic differences that mark out and *bring into being* a "this" which is different from a "that." The difference doesn't precede its notation in language: language's system of differences creates it. We don't know what a spoon is by looking at it directly; we know what a spoon is by knowing that it is not a knife or a fork, and we know what a knife or fork is by knowing that it isn't a spoon. Items do not emerge singly, but in a package or unit—like the unit of eating utensils as distinguished from the unit of gardening utensils—that is itself linguistically established; eating utensils and garden utensils are not natural kinds in the world. Knowledge of things is relational, not frontal, and the relations that matter because they are constitutive are the relations between signs, between words. We don't see first and *then* bring in words as a supplemental, secondary tool; we see through the lens of whatever vocabulary fills our consciousness, and items in the world emerge in the form permitted and demanded by that lens.

It follows that we can't "go around" language to get at things directly; we can only pass from one vocabulary that delivers the world to us in a particular shape to another vocabulary that will deliver the world to us in another particular shape. So while Orwell is right to link the deployment of a polemical vocabulary to the assertion (and perhaps imposition) of a political vision, he is wrong to think that there is a vocabulary that embodies no political assumptions at all, a vocabulary that just tells the truth, a vocabulary that will, if we attach ourselves to it, allow us to escape angled seeing and thereby neutralize politics. Orwell believes that we can arrive at that vocabulary (called by the historian of science Thomas Kuhn a "neutral observation language") by subtraction, by excising all words that "do not point to any . . . object," all words that refer to abstractions rather than concrete things, all words that are not Anglo-Saxon monosyllables. If we do this, if we clean up our language—rid it of shadings, colorings, preferences, hidden biases, and foreign influences—we will have taken, he promises, "the first step to political regeneration. . . . If you simplify your English, you are freed from the worst follies of orthodoxy." We can disarm the siren songs of fascism and communism by hewing to a vocabulary that immediately registers them as nonsense. If only it were that easy.

The Hope of Doing Without Language

Orwell's is not a new project. The idea that by purging our vocabulary we might both refine our perception and ground our actions in something more objective than words has been around for a long time. At its most extreme, as in the third book of Jonathan Swift's *Gulliver's Travels*, it amounts to a recommendation (which Orwell is close to making) that we forsake language altogether. The citizens of Swift's Lagado carry a large number of things in their packs, and when they want to "converse" they take out those things "necessary to express the particular business they are to discourse on." If you have the thing itself and stick to it, you needn't fear that its true shape will be obscured by words. Over the centuries, the project has been more seriously urged than it is by Swift, who obviously mocks it. Many learned proposals have been put forward, including the recovery of the pre–Tower of Babel language spoken by Adam and Eve in Eden (where both the human mind and its linguistic expressions were pristine and unadulterated), the construction of artificial languages like Esperanto, the construction of languages that mime and are constrained by the structure of logic (if you can only say things that are logically sound, you will be insulated from error), and the imposition of strict limits on the kind of language you can use.

One of Orwell's precursors, John Wilkins, proposed (in his 1668 "An Essay Towards a Real Character, and a Philosophical Language") the elimination from our vocabulary of redundancies (more than one word for a thing), equivocals (words that refer to more than one thing), and metaphors (words that tell you what a thing is like, not what it is). Wilkins anticipates Orwell when he predicts that these simple steps will have the salutary effect of "unmasking many wild errors that shelter themselves under the guise of affected phrases." Wilkins's contemporary Bishop Thomas Sprat is positively outraged at the harm done to learning by eloquence: "Who can behold, without indignation, how many mists and uncertainties these specious tropes and figures have brought on our knowledge?" (*The History of the Royal Society of London*, 1667).

If the uncertainties Sprat complains of could be removed

by confining ourselves to a language that did not admit them, there would be no need for argument; for argument is required only when there are competing accounts of what is the case. If everyone agreed on how a set of facts should be characterized, there would be no competing accounts and there would be nothing to argue about. And such agreement would be assured if there were a prior agreement about the correct vocabulary for stating things. If all parties were bound to a language that reflected a general perspective rather than the perspective of any one of them, bound to the kind of language Orwell, Wilkins, and Sprat urge in slightly different ways (a language much like mathematics or geometry or the digital computer), disagreement could not occur because the triggers of disagreement—conflict and uncertainty—would have been dispelled in advance. In the usual model of argument, the participants begin by talking past each other; you say this and I say that and then we engage in a give-and-take that will (it is hoped) take us to a place where we both stand on even ground and are saying the same thing. But if all parties are ventriloquists of the same language from the beginning (because they accept the constraints of the same severe linguistic regime), they are already saying the same thing and argument has no work to do.

Clearly then, *the desire for a language purged of subjectivity and political bias and the desire for an end to argument go together*; each implies the other. Establish the neutral observation language as the only acceptable linguistic currency and no one will be able to say something errant or off the wall without immediately being detected and rejected; everyone will be on the same page; the goal argument works toward—a shared understanding so complete that argument can retire from the field—will have already been reached. We will have achieved what the contemporary philosopher Jürgen Habermas calls the "ideal speech situation," a situation in which everyone has left behind his partisan desire for a self-serving outcome and offers to his fellows only "better arguments," arguments motivated not by the desire to win but by a commitment to securing universal assent among all rational interlocutors. (We shall revisit Habermas at this book's conclusion.)

The Impossible Dream

That's the antirhetorical vision, which depends, as I have said, on identifying a baseline of perception and judgment that in and of itself constitutes a barrier to the depredations language can bring about. Whether that baseline takes the form of a stripped down, no-nonsense vocabulary (Orwell, Sprat, and Wilkins), or a policing of arguments so that only the better ones get admitted to the conversation (Habermas), or the naked word of God (referred to in theological treatises as the "milk of the pure word"), it is not something we have access to; it is a utopian hope incapable of being realized by human beings.

And yet its appeal is perennial and undeniable. We would all like to believe—on the model of Winston Churchill's quip "Jaw, jaw is better than war, war"—that agreement on the facts or on policy can be reached through rational deliberation, a respectful exchange of views, a willingness to put yourself in the other fellow's shoes, better information, a spirit of compromise, et cetera. And of course that does sometimes happen. The question is, does it happen because the parties have tapped into some conceptual or linguistic common ground that in and of itself *compels* agreement—there's nothing else to say, the case could not be clearer, no room for debate—or does it happen because the parties have determined that a temporary alliance with those whose basic views they despise will further the partisan cause at this moment? (Later on, full-blown hostilities can resume.) If it's the first, the promise of true common ground is alive; if it's the second, common ground, supposedly the antidote to or check on rhetorical manipulation, is itself a rhetorical achievement and therefore temporary, fragile, and vulnerable.

I'm afraid it's the second. The commonality we occasionally achieve is nothing more (or less) than the momentary convergence of interests established locally and abandoned as soon as one of the parties sees a shorter route to the realization of its desires. (This of course is the career of coalition politics as it is practiced in the parliamentary systems of Ireland and Israel, among others.) A strategically impelled commonality is a construction, and more often than not will have to be constructed again. In this version of common ground, rhetoric is neither a value-added extra making the naturally or objectively good look a bit better nor an obstacle to clear-sightedness; rather it is necessary and constitutive; it is everything; without it, institutions, communities, crusades, reform movements, political change, and much more could not even get started. The claim is as old as the writings of the Greek rhetorician Isocrates and as new as the case Sam Leith makes for the civilizing power of eloquence in his 2012 book *Words Like Loaded Pistols: Rhetoric from Aristotle to Obama*:

> What has rhetoric done for us? Well, it has brought about all of Western civilization, for a start. What is democracy, but the idea that the art of persuasion should be formally enshrined at the center of the political process? What is law, but a way of giving words formal strength in the world, and what is the law court but a place where the art of persuasion gives shape to civil society?

Sounds good, and it *is* good, but it leaves out the darker side of the picture, the side that leads Orwell, Wilkins, Sprat, and countless others to warn against eloquence's dangers and propose remedies designed to curtail its effects. Their common fear is the one expressed early on by Aristotle, that a sufficiently skilled speaker may make the worse appear the better and so turn humankind in the wrong direction. It is as a stay against that fear that rationalists of various stripes offer methods and requirements—no metaphors, only better arguments, only simple Anglo-Saxon words, mathematical plainness, plain meaning, strict construction, a stringent literalism—in the hope that both linguistic and general disaster might be forestalled.

"General disaster" may seem hyperbolic, but here is a Minnesota court insisting that the health of society depends on the possibility of enforcing contracts according to the literal meanings of the words they contain: "Were it otherwise, written contracts would be enforced not according to the plain effect of their language, but pursuant to the story of their negotiation as told by the litigant having at the time being the greater power of persuading the trier of fact . . . and general disaster would result" (*Cargill Commission Co. v. Swartwood*, 1924). General disaster because if there is not a level of language that repels interpretative manipulation, there is no limit to the damage the rhetorician—the best storyteller—can do.

That is why Sprat calls eloquence a "weapon" and worries that virtuous persons unskilled in the art "would be exposed to the armed malice of the wicked." There has always been an intimate relationship between talking and warfare. Words are aimed, they are sent out in volleys, they are said to "strike," they feel like knife wounds in the heart, they are sprayed around like bullets. Indeed, their effect can be greater than the effect of bullets because they do internal damage to the mind and soul. We know the colloquialisms: "His arguments beat me into the ground." "Everything was clear until he began talking." "I felt I was under a spell." "He talked me to death." The aphorism "sticks and stones can break my bones, but names will never hurt me" is false. Words can eviscerate you.

Merchants of Doubt

They can even precipitate the fall of man. Leith identifies Satan as the first and best rhetorician, the archdeceiver and the father of lies. In John Milton's version of the Eden story, Satan has assigned himself the job of persuading Adam and Eve to eat the fruit from the tree of the knowledge of good and evil. In the form of a snake, he leads Eve to the forbidden tree, all the while singing its praises. But the moment Eve sees it, she recognizes it for what it is, and she says no matter what its virtues she can't eat this fruit, for "of this tree we may not taste nor touch; / God so commanded and left that command / Sole daughter of his voice" (*Paradise Lost*, bk. 9, lines 651–53).

Here it would seem is a signal instance of a bedrock utterance that is invulnerable to argument and interpretive variation; it is not ambiguous; its source bears an impeccable authority; it is complete in and of itself. Satan seems to be in a corner, confronted with a text that leaves him no room to maneuver. Can he extricate himself and find a way to get Eve to do what she knows, with total certainty, she should not do?

Piece of cake! What he does is utter a single interjection when Eve stops speaking: "Indeed?" or, in other words, "You don't say; fancy that." The apparently benign implication is that he and she should talk about it, get it clear, which suggests, ever so gently, that it wasn't clear in the first place. Simply by subjecting the divine prohibition to the mild interrogation of "Indeed?" Satan opens up a space of doubt that he then fills with alternative readings of God's utterance. He does this by varying the intentional context within which the supposedly hard and fixed words are first heard, and then pointing out that in the light of this newly thought-up intention—and there is no end of intentions that could be hypothesized—the words mean something quite different.

Eve had assumed that the God who speaks to her and Adam is both direct and benevolent; this God is looking out for them and issuing a helpful warning. Satan's first move is to invent a God who is also benevolent, but not so direct. Yes, he says, God is testing you, but what he is testing is not your obedience but your courage. He may have said "don't eat the apple," but what he meant was "do you have the guts to defy my apparent command in the hope of improving your lot": "Will God incense his ire / For such a petty trespass, and not praise / Rather your dauntless virtue?" (692–94).

No sooner has this new God—well-meaning but a bit devious—been created by Satan's words than he creates another, a God who is not well-meaning at all, but jealous of his power and authority. That God has forbidden you to eat, Satan tells Eve, because he knows that if you do, your capacities will be enlarged and he will be less able "to keep ye low and ignorant / His worshippers" (704–5). So he's either a good God who will reward you for disobeying him because he wants you to grow, or he's a not-so-good God who forbids you to eat because he wants to keep you down. Either way, disobedience seems the way to go; you should disobey him because that is what he really desires you to do, or you should disobey him because as a tyrant he doesn't deserve your loyalty. The God whose supposedly plain words Eve could confidently cite a few moments ago is gone. (How's that for a rhetorical trick?)

It doesn't matter which of Satan's multiple (and contradictory) versions of God Eve is persuaded to. What matters is that simply by listening to him, by being willing to hear his arguments, she loses her hold on the God who had always been the foundation of her thoughts and actions, and opens the way to his being replaced by an indeterminate, "iffy" thing, the meaning of whose words is suddenly debatable. I observed earlier that argument is called for only when there is doubt, that is, when certainty is unavailable. But so great is the power of argument that certainty, no matter how apparently firm, can always be unsettled by it. Satan doesn't have to sell a particular position; all he has to do is sell doubt. He is a merchant of doubt.

Merchants of Doubt is the title of a 2010 book (and a 2014 documentary) that tells the story of how a group of men, some of them distinguished scientists, dispelled the certainties that had been established by their own discipline. They persuaded a significant portion of the American public that there is no proven connection between smoking and cancer, that acid rain is harmless, that there is no ozone layer hole, that DDT is good and Rachel Carson bad, and that global warming is not occurring, or, if it is occurring, is the result of natural cycles and not of preventable human activity.

The subtitle of the book asks and promises to answer the key question: *How a Handful of Scientists Obscured the Truth on Issues from Tobacco Smoke to Global Warming.* The task the handful faced was daunting, not as daunting, perhaps, as the task facing a talking snake who is trying to convince the mother of us all to believe him rather than God, but daunting nevertheless. It would seem that no set of arguments could succeed in the face of undeniable scientific fact: "How," ask Naomi Oreskes and Erik Conway, the authors of *Merchants of Doubt*, "could the industry possibly defend itself when the vast majority of independent experts agreed that tobacco was harmful, and their own documents showed that they knew this?" (24).

The answer, simply, was "to market doubt," just as Satan did. A tobacco industry executive admitted in 1969, "Doubt is our product," because "it is the best means of competing with the 'body of fact' that exists in the minds of the general public" (34). Here the scene of persuasion is nicely defined: there's the public, whose members believe something because they have been told it by authoritative voices, including the voice of the surgeon general of the United States, and there's the mission apparently impossible that the industry spokespersons have assigned themselves—to dislodge from the public mind the set of truths it has accepted for good reason. So, how do they do it?

They don't so much dispute the science (although they do that, too) as mount a philosophical argument in the light of which the science is inconclusive and regulation premature. That argument has four steps: First, declare (correctly) that absolute or undeniable truth is not what science delivers; rather, what is taken to be true at any moment has been established by a research consensus, not by God or pure reason. Second, observe (again correctly) that a research consensus is merely the present thinking of fallible men and women, and as such it can be disrupted by the emergence of new evidence or the discovery of a flaw in the data scientists had been relying on. Third, argue that because the present consensus is subject to change and revision, it should not be the basis of a resolution to act decisively; caution is warranted. Fourth, conclude that strong government oversight is not called for; we needn't mount a campaign against tobacco use or spend money combatting acid rain or devise industry-crippling plans to deal with global warming on the basis of the not-yet-proven assumption that it is man-made.

The brilliance of this argument is that in its course the fact of consensus is turned into a liability; widespread agreement among researchers becomes a cause for suspicion; perhaps they're all just toeing a party line and closing their minds to challenges from outlying precincts; let's do more research and wait until all the evidence is in.

The sleight of hand here involves the deliberate forgetting of where the sequence began, with the acknowledgment that in science (or in any other field of investigation for that matter) all the evidence is never in. And if incomplete evidence is the inevitable condition of inquiry, you can't cite the incompleteness of evidence as a reason for failing to act on the evidence that *is* in. (You can't say we shouldn't act until all the evidence is in if you've just said that all the evidence is never in.)

Yet that is the argument that proved to be persuasive to many, in part because it was joined to an appeal that flattered the public even as it was being misled. Always remember, the public was told, that scientists aren't infallible; they can't really determine what is absolutely the case; so shouldn't we all exercise our own judgment? Here is a spokesman for the tobacco industry making just that point: "We believe that any proof developed should be presented fully and objectively to the public and that the public should be allowed to make its own decisions" (32). Saying "you be the judge" is always a good rhetorical move, especially when the "you" being deferred to doesn't know what it's talking about and can be led to any conclusion desired by a master manipulator. And that is the way, say Oreskes and Conway, that "the tobacco industry . . . and the skeptics about acid rain, the ozone hole, and global warming strove to 'maintain the controversy' and 'keep the debate alive' by fostering claims that were contrary to the mainstream of scientific evidence and expert judgment" (241).

The Escape from Doubt

What is remarkable is that after exhaustively documenting a series of massive deceptions foisted on a public that was incapable of withstanding them, Oreskes and Conway somehow believe that we can take steps to "make sure that we don't get fooled again" (248). Being fooled means being bamboozled, having the wool pulled over our eyes, and the implication of the phrase is that if we had only been more alert or less susceptible to illegitimate appeals, it wouldn't have happened. But the message of *Merchants of Doubt*, delivered over and over, is that there were no defenses against the strategies devised by the hucksters: "The industry had realized that you could create the impression of controversy simply by asking questions" (18). And once the impression is created nothing can completely remove it, not even the bringing forward of the evidence the doubters have been demanding. A significant number of Americans still believes that President Obama is a Kenyan and a Muslim, still believes that Saddam Hussein had something to do with 9/11, still believes that 9/11 was an inside job, still believes that Elvis lives.

When apparently incontrovertible evidence contrary to these beliefs is presented, it is no trick at all—or, rather an always successful trick—to discredit it, or ask for more or declare the very volume of the evidence to be a reason for doubting it. (There must be something they're hiding.) The power of an argument is not diminished by a strong and massively supported response to it; instead the argument will draw fuel and sustenance from the very fierceness with which it is resisted; knocked down, it rises again, refreshed and reenergized by the encounter, as the mythical giant Antaeus was reenergized every time he was thrown to the ground.

The lesson is one that Oreskes and Conway resist even though their analysis generates it: argument cannot be stopped in its tracks by invoking a self-authenticating reality—an absolutely perspicuous truth or a piece of brute data or an unimpeachable authority. There is no inoculation against argument's force because there is nothing to the side of argument—no cleared space of thought, science, calculation, or revelation—that will provide us with an independent measure for assessing its validity.

Although Oreskes and Conway testify on every page to the unavailability of an antidote to argument's poison, they nevertheless offer one: Trust the experts! "We can cook our own food, clean our own homes, do our own taxes. . . . But we cannot do our own science. So it comes to this: we must

trust our scientific experts . . . because there isn't a work-
able alternative" (272). As practical advice this is pretty good.
I've given it myself when insisting that the most up-to-date
knowledge in any discipline deserves our confidence in the
absence of a message from God. But Oreskes and Conway's
entire book is a record of how the invocation of expertise,
even when backed by advanced degrees, banks of data, and
official imprimaturs, was easily countered by the repeated
act of posing a simple question like Satan's "Indeed?" The
book might easily have been subtitled *How the American Public
Rejected Expert Testimony Again and Again*, and it is at the least
surprising to find that after 270 pages of documenting that
rejection, we are told we can reverse it by fiat. If "trust in
our designated experts" (273) were an efficacious action—if
trust could simply be willed and survive all assaults against
it—the events the book rehearses would never have occurred
and there would be no reason to write it. "Trust the experts"
is a recommendation without a follow-through—it's not that
easy—and so when Oreskes and Conway say that without
that trust, "we are paralyzed" and left "with nothing but confused clamor," they are unhappily right.

Well, not quite. We are left with argument, with rhetoric,
with persuasion; that is, with everything that has created the
clamor. We are left with the hair of the dog that bit us. The
only real antidote to rhetoric is rhetoric. As I write, Pope
Francis has just issued his encyclical on global warming and
poverty. It doesn't say anything that hasn't been said before
by researchers and politicians, but my guess is that because
it is the Pope who is saying it, his arguments will have an

effect greater than anything that might have resulted from all the scientists in the world issuing their own encyclical. The truth of global warming is more likely to be established by an argument from authority than by data that supposedly speaks for itself. It may seem paradoxical, but in the contest between rhetoric and truth, truth's best ally is the rhetoric it scorns. The opposition between a naked truth and the artful language that obscures it just won't hold up. Truth and everything that supposedly threatens it are inextricable. Truth independent of argument is not something we can have, and the truth we can have—the truth forged in the course of argument—may always turn out to be falsehood. What is absent, and will always be absent, is a formula or algorithm for telling the difference. An old commercial for recording tape asked, "Is it live or is it Memorex?" It's always Memorex.

Liberal Rationalism as the Way Out (Not):
Twelve Angry Men

When Oreskes and Conway express confidence in the possibility of our not being fooled in the future, they reveal themselves to be liberal rationalists—believers in a core of reason that can be made to shine through once the encrustations of custom, prejudice, fancy words, self-interest, and misinformation have been peeled away. All you have to do is institute a procedure designed specifically to get at the truth, and if the process is respected and extraneous considerations are kept out, the truth will emerge and be recognized as such by everyone.

One celebrated dramatic presentation of this rational optimism or optimism about rationality is Reginald Rose's teleplay and film *Twelve Angry Men* (1954, 1957), the story of a jury locked in a room and charged with getting at the truth about a matter of life and death. They are being asked to judge the fate of a young man accused of murdering his father with a knife. A witness testifies that he heard the two arguing and the boy yelling "I'll kill you," and then saw him running away. Another witness says that she got to see the whole thing as she was awakened by a noise and looked out her bedroom window. The boy had done a stint in reform school and been picked up by the police for wielding a knife. As the jurors enter the jury room they seem ready to convict. One juror declares that it's "obvious."

The foreman suggests taking a vote and eleven men vote "guilty," but one man, Juror #8, votes "not guilty." The others are annoyed and call him an outlier. He responds, "It's not easy for me to raise my hand and send a boy off to die without talking about it first." This is the same strategy Satan employs—let's talk about it—and the only difference between Juror #8 and the merchants of doubt whom Oreskes and Conway excoriate is that Rose enlists us as viewers in the production of the doubt Juror #8 proceeds to sow. He does this by getting us to identify with Juror #8, described in the "Notes on Characters" as "a man who sees all sides of every question and constantly seeks the truth." (In the movie he's played by Henry Fonda. Who doesn't trust Henry Fonda?) That is exactly the pose adopted by Satan and the tobacco scientists; but because in this case we like the result—the acquittal of a disadvantaged inner-city youth—we cheer as the seeds of doubt are planted and begin to grow.

The testimony of one witness is discredited by calling into question his physical ability to get to the window where he could see what he said he saw in the time he said he saw it. The testimony of the woman at the window is compromised when someone notices she was wearing thick bifocals that she would not have been wearing when she was asleep. The fatal knife wound appears to have been the result of a blow struck downward, but, as one juror points out, the boy is much shorter than his father. Another juror familiar with knife fights explains that someone like the defendant, who knew how to use a switchblade, would never have inflicted that kind of wound.

One by one the jurors change their minds, and when one of the last holdouts blurts out a stream of racist sentiments— "life don't mean as much to them as it does to us"—the others turn their back on him, labeling him the repository of the prejudices they are pledged to set aside in the search for truth. A little later he too acknowledges, reluctantly, that there is a reasonable doubt, leaving only one outlier who is now in the position Juror #8 occupied at the beginning: he is the lone minority voice. He threatens to stand firm and produce a hung jury, but then, as the others file out, he folds and says, "Not guilty." Perfect unanimity. End of argument. End of play.

Now this ending seems to mark the triumph of careful, reasoned argument over bias, misinformation, and premature judgment, the triumph of responsible deliberation over prejudice, racism, and mere rhetoric. All audiences receive the play in just that way (it is taught and performed in many high schools and colleges as a paradigmatic example of civil discourse working correctly), but in fact it is the triumph of a story told more eloquently than the stories it competes with; not necessarily a truer story, but a more persuasive one. The play is a master class in the art of slanting a narrative and stacking the rhetorical deck. Rose takes care to put all the things an audience wants to hear—be tolerant, be measured, be respectful of legal process—in Juror #8's mouth. Those in favor of conviction say things that are easily traced back to motives no one wants to acknowledge. It's a liberal setup, with all the pumps primed to deliver the requisite audience sympathy, a sympathy that makes the audience feel good about itself for having been on the right side and for being willing, like Henry Fonda—oops, Juror #8—to see all sides of every question.

It is also a setup because all the characters, except for the offstage defendant, are male and white and straight. We can imagine a remake with women, blacks, Asians, and gays playing some of the parts, but unless the changes were cosmetic (as they were in a 1997 version), the dialogue, not to mention the title, would have to be expanded to include issues and perspectives that are excluded from the sanitized liberal conversation (full of proofs and nifty logical demonstrations) audiences respond to. A play that presents itself as a lesson in how to avoid being manipulated by surfaces, verbal and otherwise, is a tour de force of manipulation. What emerges at the end is not, as Rose would have us believe, a truth that has been *revealed* by argument, but a truth that has been *created* by argument, which might just as well have created an opposing truth. (One of the jurors holding out for conviction says that the real crime is being committed right here, in the jury room; he has a point.) The same argumentative moves that bring about an outcome you like can and have been deployed to bring about an outcome you don't like—the fall of man or the victory of the tobacco companies. A merchant of doubt is a merchant of doubt even if he flies your colors.

Mark Antony and Donald Trump: I'm Just Speaking from the Heart

So we see that argument can be either celebrated as a positive heuristic leading to the discovery of truth (as the audience of *Twelve Angry Men* is pressured to believe) or deplored as an agent of "confused clamor," and we see, too, that there is no independent way of determining which it is in any instance. In either of its guises (and again they are not as distinct as many wish) no set of conditions, however carefully staged and hedged about, can resist argument's force. This is brilliantly illustrated by the most famous example of argumentative power in English literature, Mark Antony's funeral oration over the body of Julius Caesar. Antony speaks only by Brutus's and Cassius's permission and under instructions not to dwell on Caesar's virtues. Brutus speaks first and seems to win the Roman populace to the side of the conspirators by explaining his reason for killing his friend: "Not that I loved Caesar less, but that I loved Rome more." He offers to kill himself with the same dagger, but the assembled citizens cry "Live, Brutus," "Let him be Caesar," and "We are blest that Rome is rid of him." Enter Antony, who announces, "I come to bury Caesar, not to praise him," not, that is, to speak in a way that will provoke outrage against his slayers.

This is only the first of Antony's several disclaimers of rhetorical intent. I am not, he says, "disposed to stir / Your hearts and minds." Therefore I will not read Caesar's will lest it "inflame you." (But of course his hearers' hearts and minds have now been inflamed by the desire to have the will read.) Nor will I parade reasons, as Brutus did ("I speak not to disprove what Brutus spoke"). Instead, I shall "speak right on," that is, without premeditation, because that's the kind of man I am. "I am no orator, as Brutus is; / But as you know me well, a plain blunt man. . . . For I have neither wit, nor words, nor worth, / Action nor utterance, nor the power of speech / To stir men's blood." In short, I'm not trying to do anything (like persuade you); nor am I trying to get you to do anything (like rise up against Caesar's murderers). I am without artifice and speak directly from the heart with no ulterior motive.

The trick of artfully disclaiming art is one of the oldest in the book; everyone knows it ("aw shucks, I'm just a country boy") and yet it works, almost every time. One of the curious things about rhetorical strategies is that they can succeed even when those they manipulate are aware of what is being done to them. Think of the penitent husband who says, "I'm sorry, honey, and by the way, you look beautiful today." People who are being flattered know it, but they love it anyway. Knowledge, even deep knowledge, of the techniques of argument, is no defense against them. An orator can call attention to the mechanics of his performance and still be secure in the success of his art.

That is what Antony does when, in the space of a few lines, he produces an effect, denies any intention of doing so, and displaces the effect he simultaneously produces and denies onto a fictional surrogate—the person he would be were he not so woefully inarticulate. I am not eloquent, he says, but here's what would happen if I were turned into someone who was: "Were I Brutus and Brutus Antony, there were an Antony / Would ruffle up your spirits." He pictures himself playing a role he is in fact playing, imagines a response to his performance that is anything but imaginary (it is occurring now and he knows it), and describes with anatomical precision the process by which his words are at this instant entering the minds and hearts of his auditors: such an Antony as I am not would "put a tongue / In every wound of Caesar that should move / The stones of Rome to rise and mutiny." No sooner has he said that he doesn't want them to mutiny than they shout, in unison, "We'll mutiny."

This is a textbook illustration of the power of rhetoric and argument to fashion the truths that move men to action. In principle, Antony's performance is no different from Juror #8's; it's just more showy. Within a few minutes the citizens have traded in one certainty—"We are blest that Rome is rid of him"—for another: "Revenge! About! Seek! Burn! Fire! Kill! Slay! / Let not a traitor live," and had there been an opportunity for Brutus to regain the pulpit, he might well have turned the tide again. After his speech is over, Antony comments on its effect: "Now let it work. Mischief thou art afoot / Take thou what course thou wilt." Like a mighty river the course eloquence takes overflows all boundaries and overwhelms the obstacles (like common sense, common ground, pure reason, empirical fact) erected to dam or contain it.

At the moment of his rhetorical but rhetorically disclaimed triumph, Antony conjures up a vision of stones rising at the command of the Brutus he is not, an allusion to Orpheus, whose voice was so alluring that in response to it stones were moved to dance and spears thrown at him were made to turn back. Orpheus could sing his way out of anything, even Hell. In the American version of the same legend, Stephen Vincent Benét's "The Devil and Daniel Webster," the title hero is described as an orator who once "spoke against a river and made it sink into the ground"; it was said that when he went fishing, "the trout would jump out of the stream right into his pocket, for they knew it was no use putting up a fight against him." In the story, Webster defends a man who, in a moment of despair, had sold his soul to the Devil. Now the Devil wants his due and the farmer begs Webster to argue his case, which he does before a jury of villains and reprobates hand-picked by the Devil. The odds against him are long (the judge has presided enthusiastically over the Salem witch trials), but in the end the jury decides for the defendant, and its spokesman explains that "even the damned may salute the eloquence of Mr. Webster."

But as we have seen in the persons of Satan and the merchants of doubt, the damned may also *practice* the eloquence of Mr. Webster. If the power of argument can, like faith, move mountains, it can do so in the service of bad as well as good motives. Argument's strengths are also its dangers. Argument unsettles; it opens things up; it challenges and unfreezes orthodoxies; it clarifies positions, your own as well as your opponent's. (This is what we are supposed to think happens in *Twelve Angry Men*.) But argument can also work to muddy the waters or to obscure a truth, as it does in *Paradise Lost* and in the story told by Oreskes and Conway. Argument, when conducted with strength and savvy, is potent medicine; and like other potent medicines it can have side effects that are worse than any benefit it might confer. Argument can beat back the powers of Hell, as it does for Orpheus and for Daniel Webster in Benét's story, and it can also pave the road to Hell, as it does, quite literally, in *Paradise Lost*, and practically as it does in the story of the tobacco scientists.

What is common to the examples surveyed so far is that in each of them the wielder of argument succeeds in circumstances that make success unlikely. Who would have thought that Satan could so easily dislodge the word of God? Who would have thought that the tobacco scientists could effectively sow doubt in the face of what seemed to be incontrovertible evidence? Who would have thought that Juror #8 would prevail against the unanimous judgment of his fellow jurors? Who would have thought that Mark Antony could in a short time entirely reverse a recently entrenched public opinion?

And who would have thought that in the 2016 election cycle, Donald Trump would top the list of Republican presidential candidates despite the fact that (a) he had no political experience, (b) he had almost no campaign organization, and (c) he gave speeches that violated every rule in the political consultant's handbook.

That handbook will tell you that a good political speech should make policy points concisely and clearly; examples should be apt and not get in one another's way; the line of argument should be clean and crisp; the effect should be cumulative, building up to an earned conclusion. You don't want to give the impression of speaking randomly, of being all over the place, of saying whatever happens to come into your head without any care for what you just said a moment ago.

But that's exactly the impression Trump gave. His speeches had no beginnings. He just jumped in with a topic (often a hobbyhorse) and then abandoned it within seconds. He offered asides that became the main path, but only for a little while. He interrupted himself to touch and comment on his hair. He bragged about his hotels and apartment houses and golf courses and boasted that he went to the Wharton School. He recalled at length conversations with friends no one in the audience would have known or cared about. He beat up on the press; and he did all these things in no particular order and with no apparent concern for the coherence of his presentation.

This hodgepodge of anecdote, innuendo, braggadocio, and bombast led one pundit (Jack Shafer) to say, "Donald Trump talks like a third-grader." No, he talks like Michel de Montaigne (1533–1592), one of the smartest men that ever lived. Reacting against the highly structured and obviously composed writing of his predecessors and contemporaries, Montaigne announced, "I write naturally and without a plan; the first stroke of the pen just leads to a second." His prose, he said, is the "minute to minute" unfolding of "changeable" and sometimes "contradictory" notions. The key word is "naturally." I'm not of superior intelligence, Montaigne is telling his audience; I'm not coming at you with canned points; I'm just telling you what I think. Trump tells his audience, "I don't use teleprompters, I just speak from the heart." Politicians always say that, but Trump's performance breathes it.

And yet that performance has a method. Trump's artlessness, like Mark Antony's, is only apparent. Listen, for example, as he performs one of his favorite riffs. He begins by saying something critical of Mexicans and Chinese. Then he turns around and says, "I love the Mexican and Chinese people, especially the rich ones who buy my apartments or stay at my hotels or play on my golf courses." It's their leaders I criticize, he explains, but then in a millisecond he pulls the sting from the criticism: "they are smarter and stronger than our leaders; they're beating us." And then the payoff all this has been leading up to, the making explicit of what has been implied all along. "If I can sell them condominiums, rent space to them in my building at my price, and outfox them in deals, I could certainly outmaneuver them when it came to trade negotiations and immigration." (And besides, they love me.)

Here is the real message, the message that makes sense of the disparate pieces of what looks like mere disjointed rambling: I am Donald Trump; nobody owns me. I don't pander to you; I don't pretend to be nice and polite; I am rich and that's what you would like to be; I'm a winner; I beat people at their own game, and if you vote for me I will beat our adversaries; if you want wonky policy details, go with those losers who offer you ten-point plans; if you want to feel good about yourselves and your country, stick with me.

So despite the lack of a formal center or an orderly presentation, Trump was always on point because the point was always the same. He couldn't get off message because the one message was all he had.

His rivals didn't understand this until it was too late. They kept asking, "Where are the specific policies?" and "How exactly will he get Mexico to pay for that wall?" and "What about his divorces and bankruptcies?" Then they wondered why none of this negative stuff was sticking. What they didn't understand was that the old political playbook in which these questions would have some force was not the one Trump was playing by. Had he taken their questions seriously, he would have been entering a contest he didn't want to win, the contest to determine which of the candidates measured up to the traditional standards of the political process. Trump was in the act of throwing those standards out; he wasn't saying, I'm better than those guys; he was saying, those guys are up to the same old tricks, pandering to every constituency in sight; I'm not pandering to anyone, in fact I'm doing what you have always wanted to do, stick it to all of those elites who have been lording it over you for years. Of course he was himself one of those elites, and the voters knew that, but they just didn't care. They saw in Trump a big rich guy who had everything, wasn't ashamed of it, and was promising to give a piece of it to them. The fact that he never really explained how he was going to do it didn't count for anything, to the dismay of those who woke up each morning resolved to find a way to stop him. They never did.

Trump's success—incomprehensible to political comment-ators—is a twenty-first-century testimony to the truth classical rhetoricians made the basis of their pedagogy. They challenged students to make winning arguments for positions and causes it was thought no one could defend. They knew that argument could overcome any obstacle; and they knew, too, what Trump and Satan and Mark Antony and the merchants of doubt demonstrate: even in the most extreme cases, the achievements of argument are always wonderful (in the root sense of provoking wonder), especially when they are awful.

Argument's Two Faces:
Good and Bad Persuasion

The fact that the skill of argument is neither an unalloyed good thing nor a diabolically inspired bad thing, but is some-times one, sometimes the other, sometimes both, has led the friends of argument to argue for argument's "indifferent" status: it is not good or bad in itself, but can be either good or bad depending on the circumstances and the spirit in which it is deployed. Aristotle acknowledges that bad men may abuse it, but, after all, he observes, that "is a charge which may be made in common against all good things."

But this view of rhetoric/argument as a neutral instrument that can be put to both beneficial and harmful uses is entirely too cool an account of the matter for either rhetoric's ardent champions or its fierce detractors. Each of these parties has its favorite story, which, once formulated, is retold again and again through the centuries.

The positive story, rehearsed endlessly by Cicero and his followers, is one in which at the beginning of human history "men wandered at large like animals" without the benefit of an ordered system of social values. At a certain point the first master of eloquence and argument emerged and by the power of his voice (Orpheus again), he "transformed . . . wild savages into a kind and gentle folk" (Cicero, *De Inventione*). In his *Antidosis*, Isocrates is even more fulsome in his praise of argument and persuasion: "Because there has been implanted in us the power to persuade each other and to make clear to each other whatever we desire, not only have we escaped the life of wild beasts, but we have come together and founded cities and made laws and invented arts; . . . there is no institution devised by man which the power of speech has not helped us to establish." Eloquence and argument, in short, bring civilization.

But in the other, the negative story, told by Plato and a host of successors down to Orwell and beyond, eloquence and argument threaten civilization and bring epistemological anarchy ("confused clamor") by replacing the plain truth with flowery language and mesmerizing fictions.

Both stories are true.

They are stories, finally, of two kinds of persuasion, one bad and one good. Good persuasion aids in the rational sorting through of alternatives that characterizes a democratic society; participants make their points in a cooperative effort to arrive at a solution to a political or economic or military problem. "What's the best thing to do?" is the governing question. Bad persuasion is an instrument of power; participants make their points with the twin intentions of leaving the opponent with nothing to say and capturing the sympathy, not the rational agreement, of the audience. "What can I do to win?" is the governing question. But—and this is the kicker—because the resources available to the two kinds of persuasion (figures of speech, figures of sound, emotional appeals) are the same, it is difficult, to say the least, to tell the difference between them; especially since one of the strategies of the bad kind of persuasion is to present itself as the good kind, either by disclaiming any rhetorical intent (as Mark Antony does) or by larding its presentation with the trappings of rational discourse—numbered sections, words and phrases like "therefore" and "so we see"—or by repeated and theatrical invocations of Truth.

Devising a method for ensuring that the good kind of persuasion is not mistaken for or overwhelmed by the bad kind has been a project of rhetorical theorists from the beginning. Aristotle's taxonomy of the components of persuasion at once pinpoints the danger and suggests a way of neutralizing it. Proofs in discourse can, he said, be of three kinds: (1) *logos*, roughly the rational force of one's arguments in and of themselves; (2) *ethos*, the good character the speaker projects—you should believe me because of the kind of person I say I am; and (3) *pathos*, an appeal to the emotions and prejudices the speaker knows his audience to have—you should believe me because I speak to fears and desires you already feel and to values you already hold.

Of the three, *logos* is thought to be the most legitimate because it is the least tricked-up and angled, and it would be better, says Aristotle, if we could "fight our case with no help beyond the bare facts." Unfortunately, he laments, the manner of presentation greatly affects the reception of what is said, "owing to the defects of our hearers." The implication is that if only the rational capacities of men were strong enough always to guide judgment—if human faculties were rightly ordered as they were in Eden—there would be no need of an art of rhetoric at all. But given what human beings are like, the best we can do, Aristotle implies, is take care that rhetoric's potent appeals are deployed solely in the service of truth; tether the undeniable power of the ethical and pathetic to a rational purpose. The idea is that we can duly acknowledge the "defects of our hearers" without surrendering to them; we can make *ethos* and *pathos* subordinate to *logos* and not the other way around; we can have our rhetoric and not be eaten by it too.

CHAPTER 2

POLITICAL ARGUMENTS

◆————————◆

The All-Spin Zone

SOUNDS LIKE A reasonable strategy, but is it possible? Can the facts be separated from the fictions and then held up in plain view as an obstacle to distortion and manipulation? Senator Daniel Patrick Moynihan certainly thought so when he famously said, "You are entitled to your own opinions, but you are not entitled to your own facts." The idea is that the facts are the facts—they speak for themselves—and their self-declaring presence stands as a rebuke to mere opinion, founded, as it is, on nothing solid. The facts, if they are clung to, ensure that argument will not stray from the straight and narrow path.

But the "fact" that Moynihan's mantra is rehearsed by all parties to a controversy—everybody claims it just as at one time every army claimed to have God on its side—tells us that the facts do not precede argument; rather, they are fashioned in its course. Those who rehearse the mantra are saying, "My facts are the real facts, yours are only opinions." Saying that settles nothing; it merely throws down a gauntlet, the same gauntlet being thrown down by your opponent. Moynihan's pithy endorsement of fact over rhetoric is itself a piece of rhetoric, the equivalent of "so's your old man." It's a sound bite, and once sounded all the work remains to be done. That work is the work of argument, in the course of which facts do in fact become established, at least for a while. While the distinction between fact and opinion is a real one, what falls on one side or the other at any time is a matter of persuasion. You *are* entitled to your own facts if you can make them stick.

Making your facts—the facts your opponents deride as mere opinion—stick is the whole of politics, which is not a fully rational process, although neither is it irrational. It is just that the rationality must be fashioned in the course of argument; its shape is not clear beforehand. That fashioning is called, derogatively, "spin," and these days everyone is lamenting the ubiquity of spin and coming up with strategies for neutralizing it. But "spin" is a dirty word only if there is an alternative to it, only if there were a way of speaking (and thinking) that was not inflected by a challengeable political ideology, only if there were an "unspun" form of discourse to which we could, and should, turn.

No such discourse (except perhaps for the language of a computer, and that is purely formal, without substantive content) is available to us as situated human beings; the discourses that are available are all spun, and, what is worse, there is no neutral space from the vantage point of which the varieties of spin can be inventoried and assessed. In the absence of such a space, the competing spins just have to fight it out, and the fight will not be presided over by independent rules ensuring that everything is on the up and up, but by rules that are as spun as the activities they claim to order. Spin, the pronouncing on things from an interested angle, is not a regrettable and avoidable form of thinking and judging; it is the very content of thinking and judging.

So it can't be the case that what's wrong with political discourse today is spin. If there's something wrong, as most observers believe there is, it is with the form spin now usually takes. Opposing spins were spun out on a grand scale for hours and even days in the debates between Abraham Lincoln and Stephen Douglas. Long elaborations of a point were followed by even longer refutations. Each debater reached back to earlier meetings to recall large swatches of previous exchanges. Now it's all over in the millisecond it takes to deliver a sound bite—money is speech, they want to take your guns away, marriage equality, Adam and Eve not Adam and Steve. Of course there have always been sound bites, from Cato's "Carthage must be destroyed" to JFK's "Ask not what your country can do for you," but there have also been more extended forms of political back and forth, or at least there were until our political gurus became convinced that an audience's attention span lasts only a few seconds.

One of those gurus is Frank Luntz, an influential Republican pollster and consultant who has given us the "Contract with America," "death tax" as the negatively effective substitute for "estate tax," "exploring energy" as the apparently benign substitute for "oil drilling," "personalizing social security" as a warm and fuzzy substitute for "privatizing social security." These phrases, as Luntz explains in his bestselling book *Words That Work: It's Not What You Say, It's What People Hear* (2007), are bite-sized layered arguments. Those who take them in without examining them (examination is not encouraged) have internalized an entire worldview that will alter what products they buy, whom they vote for, what schools they send their children to, what attitudes they have toward law enforcement, and much else. In his writings and in his practice Luntz provides master classes in the skill of turning audiences in the direction he or his employers prefer. Yet, like Oreskes and Conway, he clings to the category of truth as something that stands above or to the side of any effort of verbal manipulation. He is an ardent Orwellian, a fan in particular of "Politics and the English Language," even though everything he says and does amounts to a refutation of Orwell's antirhetorical and antilanguage position.

Under the influence of Luntz and his colleagues in the consultant business, political conversation has become more and more stylized. By "stylized" I mean that the pros and cons are known to everyone in advance and can be rehearsed by any experienced observer in a rapid-fire, checklist summary. There may be a moment, lasting perhaps a few days or a week, when the two camps do not yet have their argumentative ducks in a row. During that period, a warrior on one side will come up with a point that seems devastating and conclusive, but it will not be long before someone on the other side thinks up a counterpoint, and the two "moves" or "thrusts" then take their place opposite each other in a formal, settled schema. When that happens, the various arguments are no longer genuine invitations to a response, as in "let me take a whack at it, then tell me what you think"; they have become "talking points"; you have yours and I have mine.

A talking point, as the phrase suggests, is designed to score points; you wield them like weapons; you say, "Take *that*," to which the other guy says, "No, you take *that*." Politicians and their proxies go on Sunday talk shows armed with talking points, and when the host asks a question, out pops a talking point whether or not it has anything to do with the question. Some radio call-in shows are structured by the canned drama of talking points: callers are asked to use one phone number if they have one view of the issue and another number if they take the contrary view. No one is surprised by anything anyone has to say. It's all by the numbers.

You Dirty Redskin!

As I write this, talking points are configuring (or reconfiguring; this is an old dispute) around the question of whether the Washington Redskins, a National Football League team, should change its name. The controversy was reignited on June 18, 2014, when the U.S. Patent and Trademark Office ruled that the name "Redskins" was a slur disparaging to a racial minority and could no longer enjoy federal trademark protection. (In 2015 a court affirmed the ruling.) Representatives of the team immediately challenged the interpretation of the name. The former coach Joe Gibbs said, "When I hear the name Redskins, I think of pride, honor, class, and respect." In response, Native American activist Amanda Blackhorse doubted that Redskins supporters like Gibbs would call her a "redskin" to her face because "they know it's offensive" (in movie Westerns the ubiquitous phrase is "dirty redskin"), and she wondered "how an NFL football team can have this name."

Arguing his team's case, the owner, Dan Snyder, brandished polls showing that a majority of Americans sees nothing wrong with the name; indeed, he added, many Native Americans don't have a problem with it. The statistics were of course disputed, but pretty soon someone said that this is not a matter to be decided by polls; no matter how many people, Native American or others, say they are not bothered by the name, the imperative is to do what's right, and what's right is not determined by a vote.

At this point the debate had shifted from an empirical to an abstract level, and an underlying opposition emerged between those who invoked the principle of antidiscrimination and those who, while agreeing that discrimination is a bad thing, invoked the principle of free private choice and derided the "nanny" state. Sure, the world might be a better place if everyone took care to refrain from giving offense, but it is not the government's job to stipulate what is and is not offensive or to specify which parties should be protected from hurt feelings; let the market sort it out. It's not just hurt feelings, was the reply; it is the right to be treated with dignity.

Dignity, came the riposte, emanates from within; you confer it on yourself and don't rely on others to shore it up by passing laws or issuing official proclamations; a truly dignified person will remain so through thick and thin, will hold his or her head high despite the slings and arrows of outrageous fortune. (This is also the argument against hate speech regulations.)

And so it goes, back and forth with everyone increasingly adept at the business of thrust and parry. And always these talking points are accompanied by hypotheticals designed to highlight the absurdity of the opponent's position. Anti-"Redskin" crusaders ask: Would you be all right with a team named the Georgia Darkies or the Miami Kikes or the Tucson Wetbacks? And on the other side: Why aren't you objecting to the Cleveland Indians or the Boston Celtics or the Minnesota Vikings or the Kansas City Chiefs or the Atlanta Braves or the Chicago Blackhawks or the Fighting Irish of Notre Dame? Once every little argument or subargument is in place along with its snarky illustrations, it's time for an episode of *Crossfire* (or some other entirely predictable pseudo-political format), where pros in this game will hit their polemical marks without breaking a sweat.

The more practiced you become in rehearsing the talking points on your side, the less likely it is that persuasion will occur, that you will change your mind. A change of mind requires that you hear something new and are provoked by it to say (if only to yourself), "I never thought of that." But you, like your opponent, have already thought of everything, have heard it all. And this hardening of conviction (called, disparagingly, by the pragmatist philosopher C. S. Peirce, the "tenacity of belief") is accelerated as you move from local questions of fact and interpretation to general assumptions about what life is and should be. In the controversy about the name "Redskins," the rubber really hits the road when you declare yourself as believing either that the government has an obligation to monitor and sanction hurtful speech (you're a big-government liberal) or that private choice, especially of expression, trumps all (you're a libertarian). Being convinced of either of these views of the responsibilities and limits of government renders you incapable of hearing arguments from the other side as anything but the progeny of error.

To Torture or Not to Torture

A similarly intractable set of oppositions informs the debate about torture, until recently a largely academic subject, but one that has increasingly been argued in public since 9/11 and the revelations about Guantánamo Bay and Abu Ghraib. Here the bottom-line opposition is between absolute right on the one hand and security and the saving of lives on the other. The starting point for debate is the "ticking bomb" scenario: a bomb that will kill hundreds or thousands or millions has been placed in an unknown location and is set to go off in hours. You have either captured the person who planted the bomb or identified a bystander who knows where it is but refuses to tell (these are two different circumstances that present different moral problems). Do you employ torture in an effort to get the information that might save innumerable lives or do you invoke the absolute moral law and say that torture is inherently evil and always wrong and must be refrained from even if the cost is terrible? (*Fiat justitia et pereat mundus*, Justice must be maintained, even if the world is lost.)

Those who opt for the second response to this dilemma initially don't have very much to say in defense of their position (although they will respond to counterarguments). Their argument is simple; torture is wrong and that's all there is to it. Those who believe that the absolutist position is naïve, unrealistic, and impossibly ideal will have lots to say, mostly in the way of the utilitarian, means-end arguments of the kind Kant and other moral philosophers deride. Yes, they will say, torture is wrong, but in extraordinary circumstances it may be necessary to save the innocent or even the world. Or they will say that while torture should always be illegal, we must acknowledge that at times of crisis we want our leaders to do things we would not ourselves do or approve by vote; those leaders will then have hands that have been dirtied so that ours can remain clean, and in the aftermath we may punish or excuse their trespass. Or they will say that unyielding moral principles are fine and good in normal situations, but normal situations themselves can be established and maintained only by extraordinary, and technically illegal, actions that are necessary and occur only rarely. Or they will analogize torture in ticking-bomb situations to self-defense: if you are justified in lashing out at someone who has cornered you in an alley, why can't you take action to neutralize an opponent who has set in motion a process that might end in the destruction of everyone and everything you love? Or they will say that because we sometimes authorize state-sponsored killing in the face of particularly heinous actions (like the cold-blooded murder of children) and torture is less harmful than killing, why can't we authorize torture in order to prevent even more heinous acts? Or they will say, let's establish conditions—very stringent—under which the state, in the person of the judiciary, can issue a "torture warrant" while maintaining the ban on torture in all unwarranted cases.

Absolutists will in turn reply that the extraordinary circumstance said to justify torture is always a trumped-up philosopher's hypothetical that never actually occurs. They will reply that consequentialist arguments for torture depend on being able to ascertain with a degree of certainty what the consequences of action or inaction will be, and we can't because the bomb may not exist, may be defective; and besides there may be other less morally culpable means of getting the desired information. They will reply that the information you do get may be unreliable because, as history tells us, "it has not been possible to make coercion compatible with truth" (John Langbein, "The Legal History of Torture," in *Torture: A Collection*, ed. Sanford Levinson, 2006). They will reply that torture never works, or, if it works in a few, one-in-a-million cases, it is both morally wrong and politically imprudent to build a general policy on the thin base of an end-of-the-world scenario that belongs more to Hollywood blockbusters than to practical calculations. They will say that if you authorize torture, either before or after the fact, in "exceptional" circumstances, the list of circumstances deemed exceptional will grow longer, and you will end up normalizing a practice everyone considers abhorrent. They will say that the analogy to self-defense fails because there is really no correspondence between the slam-bang intimacy of a back-alley assault where two persons face each other on relatively equal terms and the context of torture where all the power belongs with one party and the threat you defend against is etiolated, unclear, perhaps nebulous, and certainly yet to materialize. They will say that state killing and state torture are not equivalent: the first occurs in the context of rules of evidence, procedures that give the accused the benefit of the doubt, a system of appeals, and a resolution to execute humanely (although the idea of a humane execution is a problematic one); the second violates the rules, proceeds independently of hard evidence, hears no appeal, and, far from even pretending to be humane, begins and ends in dehumanization. And, above all, they will reply that you can't save humanity by performing acts that dehumanize both your victim and yourself; your victim is dehumanized when his powers of deliberation and rational choice are taken away by unbearable pain; he has been made a thing, and you have made yourself into a thing when you allow the desire either for revenge or security to overwhelm all your moral impulses.

Once again, the arguments line up neatly against one another, and once again underlying the specific arguments are the bottom-line, nonnegotiable convictions from which the specifics flow, the conviction on the one hand that moral right should never be compromised, and the conviction on the other hand that it is madness to cling to a purity the consequence of which might be the destruction of everything you treasure. In late 2014 the Senate Intelligence Committee issued a scathingly critical report of the CIA's torture policies and practices. The two positions I have sketched out here, with all their moving parts and mirror-like intransigencies, filled the airways within minutes.

Evidence Doesn't Do It

Convictions held at the level of underlying commitments are not vulnerable to the marshaling of evidence because it is against their background that the evidence will be received and easily discounted. In the face of what some see as incontrovertible proof, you say that polls supporting the other guy's view are faulty in design (the questions skew the results) or have surveyed the wrong population. The testimony of experts is waved away either because the expert's credentials are not good enough ("Look, he went to Podunk U") or because they are too good ("Ivy League professors are part of the establishment and their research will always mirror establishment views"). Photos are declared to be doctored; confessions are said to be coerced; documents are judged to be either fake or not dispositive; backup documents are found to suffer from the same deficiency; there is never that "aha" moment when the evidence is conclusive and there is no comeback.

Remember the demand that President Obama produce incontrovertible proof of his U.S. birthplace? The proof was repeatedly offered but it was never enough. Or think of an argument between a committed Christian and a skeptic-atheist about the resurrection of Christ. The skeptic will say that no one has ever come back from the dead; the Christian will reply that, yes, that is precisely why Jesus' doing it is evidence of his divinity. The skeptic will then ask for a materialist explanation of the miracle; the Christian will insist that it is precisely the nature of divinity to transcend materialist explanation. The skeptic will declare that nothing transcends materialist explanation—if it can't be measured or analyzed as a physical event, it doesn't exist and it didn't happen; the believer will say that this form of materialist reductionism amounts to a theology that doesn't acknowledge itself as such. At this point, which had already been reached before the back-and-forth begins, neither party will have anything left to say.

Of course, not all disagreements will exhibit the unbridgeable gulf that separates a Christian from a nonbeliever, but many disagreements, including political disagreement between entrenched partisans, will rest on a substratum of difference so deep that nothing one party could say will move the other one inch. Rather than listening to and weighing what your opponent says, you hear his words as the surface issue of deep ideological commitments you fear and despise. That is why political arguments are not concluded "on the merits": the argument is not ultimately about the specific issue that started it—the name "Redskins" or the Affordable Care Act or the reality of climate change—it is about the underlying and bedrock convictions that determine where one will come down on an issue even before it emerges.

So when a new controversy erupts—students shout down a commencement speaker or an executive resigns because of a protest against his view of gay marriage—it is easy to predict how adherents to different partisan frameworks will react and it is equally easy to predict what arguments will emerge on the other side. One side will say that the unruly students are violating the protocols of academic engagement and should be disciplined; the other will applaud the students for speaking truth to power. One side will rail against a "gay mafia" that is stifling free expression, and the other side will welcome evidence that at last corporate leaders are being held accountable for the discriminatory things they say. The calcification of political debate into arrayed phalanxes of talking points is not an aberration in political argument, it *is* political argument, at least at the present moment, and as a result political arguments go nowhere except in circles, and are rarely, if ever, won outright.

On those occasions when a political argument is won it is often because an event enters the argumentative arena sideways and produces an unexpected resolution to a dispute that promised to go on forever. For more than fifty years Cuban-American relationships were stalemated, as a U.S.-imposed embargo was firmly in place. Then one day President Obama just announced that things had changed and from now on Cuba and America were going to be friends. Almost immediately (I'd say within twenty minutes) a once-unthinkable revolution in policy became the new normal, and commentators of all stripes were saying that it had been inevitable. That of course was a judgment made in the light of hindsight; no one would have called it inevitable the day before Obama spoke.

An equally dramatic and unanticipated political turn-around altered the status of the Confederate flag after years of controversy about its meaning and its place in the political landscape of twenty-first-century society. The right of the flag to exist was not at issue; nor was the right of a private individual to display it. The issue was the displaying of the flag by a state in a manner that could be taken as an endorsement of its history. As usual, the arguments pro and con were styl-ized. It's a symbol of prejudice, hatred, and injustice, said one side. No, it's a symbol of southern heritage and states' rights, said the other. Yes, the rights of states to secede and engage in treasonous acts, was the riposte. No, it's treason when a government dictates what symbols its citizens are allowed to cherish. And on and on, it would seem forever.

Then in 2015 a young white man walked into a black church in Charleston, South Carolina—a state that flew the Confederate flag on its capitol building—and after joining the worshippers in prayer, pulled out a weapon and killed nine of them. It turned out that he had posed with a Confederate flag on several websites. That was enough (who could have pre-dicted it?) to tip the balance. Within hours everyone, from the governor of the state to its two senators to corporations like Walmart, was insisting that the flag come down. Although rallies in support of the flag were held (mostly by the KKK), the game was over, just like that. And it may be that there will be a spillover effect; some are drawing an analogy to the name "Redskins," asking, if South Carolina and Walmart have dis-carded a tainted symbol, why shouldn't a football team that plays in the nation's capital do the same thing?

It is important to emphasize that the effect of the Charleston tragedy on the Confederate flag debate was neither predictable nor inevitable. There was a ready-made argument available that counsels against drawing a far-reaching conclusion from an isolated incident that probably had more to do with an angry young man's feelings of frustration and inadequacy than with the symbol he happened to associate with his cause; after all (the argument would continue), not everyone who waves the Confederate flag at NASCAR races is going to go out and kill African Americans; let's keep some proportion here! That argument might have derailed the let's-get-rid-of-the-flag train, but it didn't.

No general conclusions, however, should be drawn. The next effect of a political turn will be as much a surprise as this one. Some liberals and progressives hope that what happened in Charleston may be the final straw that breaks the back of the gun lobby. But equally horrific incidents—Columbine, the shooting of Gabby Giffords, Newtown, even Oklahoma City and now San Bernardino—have failed to be that straw; if you are waiting for outrage at gun violence to turn the political tide, don't hold your breath. If it happens it will be by a route no one had anticipated. When the Boy Scouts of America won the right in court to exclude homosexuals it was not anticipated that the organization would be weakened by its triumph, a triumph it has now overruled on its own, first by admitting gay scouts, and then, in 2015, by allowing gay scout leaders. The gaining of the right to discriminate led (indirectly, to be sure) to the ending of discrimination. You can never tell.

Elections and Courts Don't Do It

So arguments in and of themselves don't end political debates, and events entering the arena of argument from the outside don't end political debates necessarily, although they may. The career of argument is incalculable; there is no formula either for advancing it or for determining where it is likely to go next. There are, however, procedural moments that mark the end of argument much as a bell marks the end of a round in a boxing match. Elections serve this function, at least formally. When a candidate is elected or a referendum passes, the matter is resolved. The merits of the candidates are no longer being debated; one policy has been preferred to another and is now the law of the state.

But of course the arguments do not end; they just continue in a slightly different form. Arguments about the victorious candidate's performance replace arguments about his or her qualifications. Arguments about the consequences of the newly ratified policy replace arguments about whether it should be adopted. Elections are mere pauses in the forensic wars; they decide something (who shall be called president or senator), but the underlying conflicts continue unabated. And even in those areas where an election is decisive, it is unlikely that argument in the sense of *logos*—the back-and-forth of rational propositions—carried the day. Perhaps it played a role, but roles will also have been played by the personalities of the candidates (ethos), or by advertising campaigns that arouse fears (pathos), or by a low or high turnout, or by name recognition, or by a half dozen other things that converge at a particular moment to push one party or policy across the finish line.

A similar mixture of conclusiveness and inconclusiveness characterizes the work of the courts—another device of procedural closure—where argument has always been considered the main currency. A high court decision may establish the law of the land and yet may leave the issue in dispute fully alive in the cultural conversation. *Brown v. Board of Education* (1954) declared that because separate is not really equal, the Jim Crow practice of keeping the races apart in public schools, public eating places, public transportation, public washrooms, and public swimming pools was unconstitutional. But for years afterward, the battle continued as southern states devised a number of strategies (poll taxes, literacy tests, so-called private schools) designed to blunt and delay the effects of the ruling.

The argument that the *Brown* court only appeared to settle had been raging at least since the *Dred Scott* decision (1857), in which Chief Justice Roger Taney (in)famously declared that negroes "had for more than a century been regarded as beings . . . so far inferior that they had no rights which the white man was bound to respect." Although a civil war was fought in part to reverse this judgment and although the Fourteenth and Fifteenth amendments directly repudiated it, the assumptions underlying Taney's pronouncement have not lost their force and reappear in the debates about affirmative action and "forced bussing," and in controversies over the claims of some scientists that the differences between the IQ scores of whites and African Americans have a genetic basis.

One might have thought that the election of Barack Obama as president of the United States would have put an end to these disputes (you don't elect someone you regard as congenitally inferior to the highest office in the land, twice), but from the beginning of his tenure Obama has been faced with serial accusations: he is not an American citizen (a significant percentage of Republicans believe this), his SAT scores were very low (they have not been released), he did not attend Columbia University as an undergraduate (no one remembers him, we are told), he did not attend Harvard Law School, or, if he did, his grades were terrible, and he was the beneficiary of the worst kind of affirmative action when he was made editor of the law review. Taney's arguments about the natural inferiority of the negro may have been overruled—by the courts, by constitutional amendments, by a war—but they still flourish, and the spirit informing poll taxes and literacy tests (let's make it as hard as possible for blacks to vote) now animates the recent, successful efforts to require that voters produce government-issued identity cards. It would seem that old arguments never die; they just get recycled.

The Improbable Triumph of Same-Sex Marriage

But even this general rule that I have just minted—nothing ever really gets resolved in the world of political argument—has its exceptions. In marked contrast to the persistence of arguments about race, the arguments about same-sex marriage seem to be over, even though those against it continue to voice protests. In 1996 only 27 percent of Americans favored same-sex marriage. Now, in 2015, the number is over 60 percent and climbing. How has this happened? In part because of a 2013 Supreme Court decision (*United States v. Windsor*) that declared the Defense of Marriage Act (DOMA) unconstitutional. That act, passed in 1996, defined marriage as a formalized relationship between a man and a woman. When Edith Windsor's partner, Thea Spyer, died in 2009, Windsor claimed the federal tax exemption allowed to surviving spouses who have inherited the deceased's estate. (She and Spyer had been married in Canada in 2007.) The Internal Revenue Service, citing DOMA, denied the claim. Windsor paid $363,053 in estate taxes and then in 2010 filed a lawsuit seeking a refund. She argued that DOMA singled out married same-sex couples for "differential treatment compared to other similarly situated couples without justification."

This argument would have had little, if any, traction thirty years ago because under the understanding then prevailing (and it had prevailed for a very long time) this kind of "differential treatment" needed no "justification" because the difference—between the state-certified union of a man and a woman and the mere cohabitation of persons of the same gender—was obvious, indisputable, and a fact of nature, and in relation to that fact, the two couples are not in any way "similarly situated." ("Similarly situated" begs the question: "similarly" is the issue and it cannot be resolved by simply repeating the word.)

This argument from nature or natural morality goes back at least as far as *Reynolds v. United States* (1879) when the court ruled against the argument made by a Mormon that he had engaged in plural marriage—polygamy—in response to the dictates of his religion. The court pointed out that the law recognizes only monogamous unions, and besides—and this is the real point—"Polygamy has always been odious among the northern and western nations of Europe . . . and was almost exclusively a feature of the life of Asiatic and of African people." In other words, we are white Christians and we don't do that sort of thing. The Mormon defendant had relied on the Free Exercise clause of the First Amendment, which has at times been interpreted as allowing an exception to generally applicable laws when the conduct at issue is religiously inspired. But, said the court, "there has never been a time in any State of the Union when polygamy has not been an offense against society . . . and it is impossible to believe that the constitutional guaranty was intended to prohibit legislation in respect to this most important feature of social life." That is to say, polygamy is so unnatural, so obviously against the dictates of morality (at least the morality of Western white Protestant societies), that it is unthinkable that the Constitution could be read to permit it; no way the Founders could have had *that* in mind when enacting the Free Exercise clause, even if that might seem to be the plain meaning of their words.

Exactly the same reasoning—deeply entrenched morality determines the legal status of an act—was put forward by the majority in *Bowers v. Hardwick* (1986), the case that affirmed Georgia's antisodomy law. Proscriptions against "acts of consensual sodomy," the court wrote "have ancient roots," the same roots that proscribe plural marriage. Responding to the objection that the only basis for the law is the "belief of a majority of the electorate in Georgia that homosexual sodomy is immoral," the court replied that the "law . . . is constantly based on notions of morality" and therefore we do not agree that "majority sentiments about the morality of homosexuality should be declared inadequate."

The "we" in this last sentence did not include Justice John Paul Stevens, who, in dissent, made exactly the opposite point: "The fact that the governing majority in a state has traditionally viewed a particular practice as immoral is not a sufficient reason for upholding a law prohibiting it." Justice Harry Blackmun, another dissenter, drove Stevens's point home: "A State can no more punish private behavior because of religious intolerance than it can punish such behavior because of racial animus." Law, in Stevens and Blackmun's view, is not an instrument of anyone's morality or religion; rather it is an instrument for safeguarding the liberty of all the citizens who live under it, even when some of them choose to exercise that liberty in ways the majority finds objectionable. In its zeal to honor traditional morality, the court, Justice Blackmun exclaims, fails "to comprehend the magnitude of the liberty interests at stake."

It might look as if what we have here is an opposition between morality—homosexual sex is abhorrent to nature—and abstract principle—the right of individuals "to choose for themselves how to conduct their intimate relationships" (Blackmun). But there is morality and principle on both sides. The liberty principle invoked by Blackmun and Stevens follows from the morality of classical liberalism, which substitutes for the authority of an overarching moral/religious framework the prime value of individual choice unconstrained by directives from an official orthodoxy. Liberal theory says that it is not the business of the state to tell its citizens what to believe or what to say or how to order their intimate relationships; rather the state exists for the purpose of protecting the free choice of autonomous individuals from external coercion, whether it comes from the government or the church or an overweening majority. The liberal state, the legal philosopher Ronald Dworkin explains, does not declare or enforce "any particular conception of the good life or what gives value to life." Live and let live should be the rule as long as no one is hurt in the process. In the words of Immanuel Kant, "Each may seek his happiness in whatever way he sees fit, so long as it does not infringe upon the freedom of others to pursue a similar end."

It is this morality of liberty and equal treatment that the dissenters in *Bowers* oppose to the morality of religious orthodoxy, which had held sway for more than a hundred years. They lose. But seventeen years later, in *Lawrence v. Texas* (2003), they win; the dissenting view becomes the majority view and the majority view the dissenting view. In that case, the court declared that "profound and deep convictions accepted as ethical and moral principles do not answer the question before us." That is to say, those are not the kind of arguments we pay attention to here, although they were the arguments that previously had the status of "goes without saying." Now the argument that goes without saying (although it is here officially said) is that "liberty gives substantial protection to adult persons in deciding how to conduct their private lives in matters pertaining to sex." The reversal is marked, as it seldom is in the law, by a formal reversal: "*Bowers* was not correct when it was decided and is not correct today. . . . *Bowers v. Hardwick* should be and now is overruled." Or, in other words, those were the wrong arguments.

Bounded-Argument Spaces: How Scalia Foresaw the Slippery Slope

By declaring that a set of arguments once thought to be canonical is no longer respectable, the *Lawrence* majority illustrates that the law is what I call a "bounded-argument space." A bounded-argument space is one in which the arguments that can be made and the arguments that just won't fly are formally identified and known to everyone working in the field. That identification of acceptable and unacceptable arguments is not fixed; what is fixed is the fact of the two categories. When there is a change (brought about in any number of ways) the categories remain, but what fills them is different.

The *Lawrence* court announces such a change when it declares (there is no other word for it) that moral principles do not answer the question before us, even though those same principles had presided over the enterprise for a very long time. Before, one could invoke moral principles and have them determine legal arguments. Now moral principles are out and liberal principles—fairness, equality, liberty, choice—are in.

The question is, how did this revolution occur? How were

the terms of the debate about same-sex marriage reconfigured so that the old arguments against it were suddenly of no effect? The *Lawrence* decision, and the decision in *Romer v. Evans* (which in 1996 found Colorado's antisodomy legislation animated by an "animosity toward the class affected" rather than by any legitimate governmental purpose), are not the whole story. The whole story includes, but is not limited to, the Stonewall riots of 1969; the first gay pride march in 1970; the removal in 1973 of homosexuality from the list of mental disorders presented in the DSM (*Diagnostic and Statistical Manual of Mental Disorders*); the activism that grew out of the AIDS crisis of the '80s; the public coming out of Ellen DeGeneres in 1997; the prominence and public acceptance of "out" gay actors such as Ian McKellan, Derek Jacobi, Jody Foster, Nathan Lane, Lily Tomlin, Neil Patrick Harris, David Hyde Pierce, Gillian Anderson, Rupert Everett, Zachary Quinto, and Ellen Page; the now familiar and almost casual inclusion of gay characters on popular sitcoms; the fact that the California Proposition 8 case was argued and won by two prominent lawyers (David Boies and Theodore Olson) on opposite sides of the political fence; and, above all, the substitution for the old rallying cry of "gay rights" (vulnerable to the charge that the rights sought were "special") of the more defensible, indeed unanswerable in liberal terms, rallying cry of "marriage equality."

"Marriage equality" is a wonderfully resonant phrase (it is worthy of Frank Luntz), but like "similarly situated" it begs the question it peremptorily answers. The core of the debate, after all, is whether a union of same-sex partners can be legally called a marriage. Logically, you don't settle the debate by just bestowing the name "marriage" on such a union and then declaring it equal to the other form of marriage. Of course it is equal once the term "marriage" has been applied to both, but, again, that is the issue: Should the traditional definition of marriage, unchallenged for centuries, be discarded or stretched? "Marriage equality" is a sleight of hand parading as an argument. But because the parading has been immensely successful, it now *is* an argument, one that supports and mirrors Edith Windsor's argument that laws against gay marriage single out same-sex couples for "differential treatment compared to other similarly situated couples without justification." The justification that would have made the differential treatment a matter not of unfairness, but of nature and the-way-things-just-are, is no longer respectable.

To be sure, there are some who still proclaim the old arguments, but they are quickly becoming relics comparable to those who believe in an Earth that is flat or in a universe with Earth at its center. Justice Antonin Scalia was right when he predicted in his dissent to *Lawrence* that the majority decision made gay marriage inevitable. Noting that according to the majority the case "does not involve" the issue of homosexual marriage, Scalia snorted, "Don't you believe it," for "if moral disapprobation of homosexual conduct is 'no legitimate state interest' . . . what justifications can there possibly be for denying the benefits of marriage to homosexual couples?" As Scalia recognized, the slippery slope had already been slid down, and the slide was complete in 2015 with the 5–4 decision in

Obergefell v. Hodges and Justice Anthony Kennedy's ringing declaration that same-sex couples seek "not to be condemned to live in loneliness" and ask only for "equal dignity in the eyes of the law," a request, he concludes, we cannot refuse because "the Constitution grants them that right." And so it does, from now on. That argument is done.

Or, to be more precise, the argument has been cut off and replaced by a judicial fiat. That, at least, is the contention of Justice Scalia, who fails to find in Kennedy's majority opinion "even a thin veneer of law." Law for Scalia means the unfolding of the democratic process, which he understands as the give and take of argument leading to a vote that will determine, at least for the time being, which of the contending parties in a controversy has been more persuasive. The matter is temporarily settled, but the losing side, Scalia observes, has the consolation of knowing that "an electoral loss can be negated by a later electoral win." The difference between an electoral win and a Supreme Court win is that the former is a moment in a history that can take a new direction the next time the people enter the ballot box, while the latter is fixed unless a later version of the court overrules its previous holding, something that occasionally happens, but not something you can count on.

Until Kennedy pronounced in *Obergefell*, the debate about same-sex marriage proceeded in the usual way: "Individuals on both sides of the issue passionately . . . attempted to persuade their fellow citizens to accept their views." This back and forth, says Scalia, "displayed American democracy at its best" and was an example of "how our system of government is supposed to work." What disturbs Scalia is not the result reached by the majority, but the fact that it is a result handed down by five justices rather than by the democratically expressed will of the people in the course of public argument. He declares it of no importance to him "what the law says about marriage"—he is not coming down on either side of the substantive question—but it is "of overwhelming importance" how the law came into being. The logic of democracy demands that "the public debate over same-sex marriage must be allowed to continue," but, Scalia laments, the "Court ends this debate" in what amounts to a "Judicial Putsch."

Some might say that the Scalia imperative—let the people, not five appointed jurists, decide—is one he himself violates, when in *D.C. v. Heller* (2008) he sets aside the democratically arrived at decision of the District of Columbia to (in effect) ban the use of handguns by private citizens. But Scalia could easily reply—and would reply were he still alive, he needs no help from me—that the District's ordinance interfered with a right granted to its citizens by the Second Amendment, and if the Second Amendment has spoken, no argument can stand against it.

Of course, it could be argued (as I in fact have) that Scalia's reading of the amendment is tortured and strained, but that would be an argument about the precise scope of the right granted by the amendment, not an argument that we shouldn't look to the text of the Constitution at all and instead take our direction from abstractions like *identity, intimacy, aspiration*, and *dignity*, all words Kennedy uses, and words that bear the mark of the new-age sensibility Scalia derides when he refers contemptuously to the majority opinion's "showy profundities." Scalia is fine with shutting down argument as long as it is the constitutional text that does it. He is not fine with shutting down argument because five justices declare that morality has now acquired a new and final shape that they are uniquely equipped to see. Somehow these hubristic jurists "are certain" that the Fourteenth Amendment has bestowed on them "the power to remove questions from the democratic practice" whenever their "judgment" tells them that a question has been settled forever.

Scalia's position in *Obergefell* is of a piece with his originalism, the theory of legal interpretation with which he will always be identified. Originalism comes in two versions— textualism and intentionalism—but in either version the core assertion is the same: interpretation is an act in which the past sets the agenda for the present. Should a question arise about the constitutionality of a statute, you first figure out what the Constitution says and then apply what the Constitution says to the present dispute. You don't start with the answer you prefer—either the statute is constitutional or the statute is unconstitutional—and then massage the Constitution's text until it can be said to support that answer. That's "living constitutionalism," and it is what both textualists (like Scalia) and intentionalists (like me) oppose, because they believe that detaching the text from its original meaning is to abandon interpretation—which, logically, must have an object that is prior to its operations—in favor of a manipulation that has no constraints except the constraint of what the interpreter (not really one) desires to find. The spirit of living constitutionalism was pithily captured by the philosopher Richard Rorty, who once remarked that interpretation is the act of beating the text into the shape that best serves one's present purposes.

That is what Scalia accuses Kennedy and his colleagues in the majority of doing: they affirm a moral perspective they like and heap scorn on a moral perspective they dislike, and in the course of this can't-fail exercise they untether themselves from the constitutional text, even as they (rhetorically) invoke it. That's all there is to it, Scalia complains: the majority justices are no longer "functioning as *judges*, answering the legal question whether the American people had ever ratified a constitutional provision that was understood to proscribe the traditional definition of marriage." Instead they are functioning as an "unelected committee of nine" intent not on interpreting the Constitution, but on revising it in accordance with their parochial moral vision. They are not accepting the task of trying to determine what the framers meant, a task that is necessarily argumentative because words don't speak for themselves (if they did, both argument and interpretation would be superfluous); they are engaging in the self-indulgent pleasures of "inspirational pop-philosophy." Rather than arguing about what the Constitution means, they're just making it up as they go along.

This is strong, over-the-top language and Scalia knows it, and he knows too that what he says in this brief dissent will be memorable. People will quote it (they are already doing so) and include it in the list of Scalia-isms (the judicial equivalent of Yogi Berra-isms) that in the future will be rehearsed again and again. I cannot help believe that this is intentional, and that it is Scalia's way of ensuring that the arguments he has made in a losing cause will last longer and shine with more brilliance than the arguments—in his view barely arguments at all—that won.

But he did lose, and right now the questions that remain are questions of application: first, whether the arguments that won same-sex unions the name "marriage" will be extended to polygamy (I can see no legal bar to that happening); and, second, whether gay marriage opponents will be able to do an end run around *Obergefell* by arguing that the Free Exercise clause of the First Amendment permits religiously committed florists or caterers or photographers to withhold their services from gay couples. (I can't stop them from marrying, but I shouldn't be forced to be a party to their sin.) Recent Supreme Court decisions affirming the "rights of conscience" open this avenue and it will certainly be pursued, but I would bet that in the end, the tide will have turned too conclusively, and the same-sex marriage victory will be complete and long-lasting.

Abraham Lincoln, the Anti-Liberal

As my two examples show, the relationship between cultural change and legal argument does not always have the same trajectory. In the case of the civil rights revolution, the law was ahead of the culture and made arguments many in society were not ready to accept. In the case of the gay rights revolution, the law was catching up with the culture and made arguments that were already in ascendancy. The general point is that in politics, arguments alone don't win the day; the time must be ripe, the setting must be favorable, and the slogans (like "marriage equality") must be catchy and stand as arguments in their own right.

Indeed, the phrase "arguments alone" is misleading, for it suggests that an argument can have force independent of the occasion of its use. In fact arguments—even arguments on the highest formal level, such as arguments for equality and liberty—don't point in a single direction or belong to one side in a context of dispute, but take on the substantive coloring of the side that appropriates them. In the battle over gay rights, the arguments for equality and liberty did yeoman work; why shouldn't gays and lesbians have the same freedom of choice accorded to heterosexuals? You may not like the form of "intimate relationship" your neighbor chooses, but he may not like yours. Why should either of you impose a moral vision on the other? Live and let live. Put that way, the argument for freedom of choice would seem to be a reliable instrument for the expansion of liberty and the diminishing of discrimination.

But exactly the same argument was used by Stephen Douglas to justify maintaining the discrimination (too weak a word) inherent in the institution of slavery. In his debates with Abraham Lincoln, Douglas preached the gospel of self-government: "I look forward to the time when each State shall be allowed to do what it pleases. If it chooses to keep slavery forever, it is not my business, but its own; if it chooses to abolish slavery, it is its own business, not mine. I care more for the great principle of self-government . . . than I do for all the negroes in Christendom." Or in other words, live and let live and don't impose your moral convictions on your neighbor.

Lincoln's reply put him in the company of the majorities that won the day in *Reynolds* and *Bowers*, that is, on the side of Christian morality and against liberal values. He saw the argument for equality and freedom of choice not as an extension of a "great principle" as Douglas did, but as a device for avoiding and evading the paramount issue of what is right and what is wrong. Judge Douglas, Lincoln explained, "has said that 'he don't care whether [slavery] is voted up or down,'" but that makes sense only if it is agreed that slavery is not wrong: "Any man can say that who does not see anything wrong in slavery, but no man can logically say it who does see a wrong in it; because no man can logically say he don't care whether a wrong is voted up or down." In short, states' rights cannot be extended to the point where the states have a right to do wrong.

The liberal response to Lincoln, Douglas's response, is that matters of moral right and wrong are best left off the political table, because, in the absence of a neutral, objective formula for adjudicating competing moral visions, conflict will inevitably break out, and if we want peace, it's better to enforce the principle of individual choice and allow the competing visions to exist together in the political space. Lincoln's counterresponse to that reasoning (he borrows from Matthew 12:25) is well known and proved prophetic: "A house divided against itself cannot stand."

I introduce the Lincoln-Douglas debates because they complicate any attempt to draw a straight line between a form of argument and a political position. Douglas is pushing a states' rights argument (as did prosegregationists a hundred years later) because it supports the outcome he desires. In recent years advocates of both gay rights and the decriminalization of marijuana have made states' rights arguments because they felt that a federal law embracing the outcome *they* desired was unlikely. Although the states' rights argument has often been thought to belong to conservatives, it belongs to the side that manages to put it in the service of its agenda. You don't begin with a principled argument and then deduce from it a substantive position; you begin with a substantive position and then you look around for a so-called principled argument that might help you to implement it. The House Speaker Tip O'Neill famously said, "All politics is local." What I'm saying is that all argument is local, which means that all argument is rhetorical. Although the philosophical tradition proclaims a distinction between the giving of arguments, which belongs to *logos*, and the production of rhetorical effects, which belongs to *pathos* and *ethos*, and elevates the former over the latter, everything is really on the rhetorical side. Arguments can migrate from one political party to another depending on where a rhetorical advantage is spied; everything is always on the wing, capable of metamorphosing into its opposite; reversal and transformation, not resolution and stability, are the order of the argumentative day; nothing stays fixed; everything is ultimately up for grabs.

I Was Blind, but Now I See

There is, however, one route by which the fluidity of argument can be arrested: conversion. Conversion—from the Latin *convertio*, to turn or reverse direction—differs from ordinary, everyday persuasion in that what one is persuaded to is not a point, but a vision. Arguments (especially in law) proceed step by step; if x, then y; given these facts, this judgment. Conversion occurs at once, in a woosh (although the pressures that lead to conversion may have been building for a time), and its effects are not limited to a single issue or question. I observed earlier that most arguments, political and otherwise, are not about the issues that are on the table; they are about the worldview or deeper-than-deep commitments that underlie and give shape to the issues that are on the table. Conversion occurs at the level of those commitments.

The classic case is the conversion of Saul of Tarsus. Saul had been a persecutor of Christians until, as he made his way to Damascus, "suddenly there shined round about him a light from heaven: And he fell to the earth, and heard a voice saying to him, 'Saul, Saul, why persecutes thou me? I am Jesus whom thou persecutes'" (Acts of the Apostles, 9:3–5). At that moment Saul's "eyes were opened," but he could not physically see until Ananias, sent by Jesus, put hands on him three days later, and "there fell from his eyes as it had been scales: and he received sight forthwith, and arose, and was baptized" (9:18). What his eyes were opened to was the truth he had long resisted, that Jesus was the Messiah; and once that truth filled his consciousness, the world appeared different in all its particulars, and his behavior completely changed and changed immediately: "And straightway he preached Christ to the synagogues, that he is the Son of God" (9:20). It is then that Saul becomes Paul, an entirely new man whose inner transformation transforms everything else in his life.

Conversion does not require a heavenly revelation. My wife became a vegetarian immediately after seeing a movie about the mistreatment of animals. German youths reportedly committed suicide after reading Goethe's *The Sorrows of Young Werther*. Frankie Valli decided to become a pop singer the night his mother took him to a Frank Sinatra concert. Dan Snyder might meet a Native American in a bar or a steam room and be so struck by what he hears that he immediately exclaims, "'Redskins'? What was I thinking?" I once heard a former white supremacist being interviewed, and he explained that he was now a *former* white supremacist because he heard the leader of his group include persons with cleft palates in the list of "defectives" who would be expelled or eliminated when the battle was finally won. It so happened that his daughter had a cleft palate. The result? Instant disaffection and conversion, and a new career as the denouncer of the beliefs he had previously held.

Typically, conversion is experienced as an instantaneous transformation—"I was blind, but now I see"—but often the moment will have been a long time coming. The historian and public intellectual Gary Wills began his public life as a protégé of the conservative icon William F. Buckley Jr., but differences between the two emerged in the context of the civil rights movement and the Vietnam War. When Buckley's journal, *National Review*, refused to publish a piece of Wills's on the war, the break, and his migration to the "enemy party," was complete. In recent years politicians on both sides of the aisle have crossed over to take on the label they had previously scorned. Usually they say that for a while they took a position here and there that was not endorsed by the party, but considered themselves still to be solidly in the fold. But then, as the instances of departure from the party line accumulated, they realized that they had wandered farther away than they had thought, and were now living somewhere else politically. The change in affiliation was merely the formal recognition of something that had already happened. There is a roster of such "ideology conversions": Whittaker Chambers, Irving Kristol, Norman Podhoretz, Charlton Heston, Ronald Reagan, David Mamet, and David Horowitz (to name just a few) all grew increasingly uncomfortable with their colleagues on the left and the positions they espoused, and ended up becoming stalwart and fierce conservatives. They were born again.

As these examples illustrate, conversion—being persuaded to a vision—does not occur piecemeal. It's the total package, the whole ball of wax. You don't assent to a single proposition and then to another and another, seriatim, but to an entire worldview. If you have been persuaded to a point—"yes, I concede that"—the effect of the persuasion may be short-lived; you were forced to the wall by a skillful debater and when the pressure of the experience is relaxed you snap right back to your original position. But if you are persuaded to a vision—if the deep assumptions that deliver your world have been flipped—the effect will be long-lasting, comprehensive, and intense; that is why converts are often so zealous in their commitment to the faith and in their resolve to live it out at every moment of their lives.

Foundationalism and Antifoundationalism

Now, strictly speaking, conversion does not belong in a book about argument because its occurrence means the end of making points on the way to a conclusion. In the instant of conversion, the conclusion ("revelation" would be the better word) will already have been arrived at, and the points still to be made reside on the edges where the newly held comprehensive truth is being applied to particular instances. Conversion is what argument aims for, but never finally achieves; indeed the achievement of so deep a clarity would spell the end of argument because there would be no work for it to do. If something is held to be certain—either because of its authoritative source or because of the absence of a counterthesis opposed to it—argument is beside the point or frivolous or irresponsible or a mistake (as Eve's fall into argument at the invitation of Satan is a mistake).

It follows that the range of argument—the area in which argument appropriately and fruitfully operates—depends on how many things are certain or at least capable of being rendered certain and how many things are doubtful, that is, available to different and incompatible accounts. In the tradition inaugurated by Plato, certainty attaches to self-evident propositions ("we hold these truths to be self-evident"), mathematical proofs, and impartially confirmed scientific calculations; everything else is at best only probable or contingent and it is only in the realm of the probable and contingent that arguments do indispensable work. The point is made by Chaim Perelman and Lucie Olbrechts-Tyteca in their magisterial reformulation of classical rhetoric: "The very nature of deliberation and argumentation is opposed to necessity and self-evidence, since no one deliberates where the solution is necessary or argues against what is self-evident." It follows then that "the domain of argumentation is that of the credible, the plausible, the probable, to the degree that the latter eludes the certainty of calculations" (*The New Rhetoric: A Treatise on Argumentation*, 1969).

How large is that domain? Proponents of a long-honored philosophical stance—often called foundationalism—want it to be very small. A foundationalist is someone who would anchor thought, communication, and action in some acontextual, suprahistorical invariant—either an authority (such as God) or a natural law (a law not made by men) or a procedure (empirical observation or scientific verification) or a value (equality, liberty, autonomy, reason, truth). The idea is that the apparent heterogeneity of the world as we experience it, with its kaleidoscopic array of meanings, interpretations, and preferences, can be reduced to order if everything that is proposed is brought before the bar of the foundational authority—not an item in the field of argument but existing above it in a transcendent position—and judged either to be in conformity with that authority or to be untethered to it and therefore without ground.

An antifoundationalist is someone who denies the availability to human beings of any such tethering foundation and who says that whatever gives our assertions and actions

weight and validity, it can't be that. It's not that antifounda-
tionalists give up on certainty (as a practical matter) or on
pronouncing something to be true or good; it's just that for
the antifoundationalist, "good," "true," and "certain" are
contextual judgments that have a local, not a universal, force.
An antifoundationalist will acknowledge that procedures for
determining what is true and standards for declaring what is
good do exist, but will insist that those procedures and standards hold only for the communities that for whatever reasons
(and there can be many) have established them as normative
currency. (The person who insists on the local status of truths
will not be led by this insight to doubt or relativize the truths
he holds. There is no relationship between the account—
foundational or antifoundational—of your convictions and
the strength or weakness of your commitment to them.)

What is not available (again, at least to human beings)
is a normative currency that holds across all communities,
contexts, and cultures. In a foundationalist vision, change is
always in the direction of linking up more securely with the
transcendent ground; we progress in an increasingly enlight-
ened way toward a union with Truth (here the model might
be scientific progress as it is popularly understood). In an
antifoundationalist vision, change occurs when a community
experiences a shift—unpredictable and comprehensible only
in hindsight—in the norms and protocols within which judgments are made. When the work of abstract artists like Braque
and Picasso first appeared, it was declared by the tastemakers
then in power not to be art. Later that same work came to be
regarded as the very model of what art is. Later still the pen-

dulum swung back in the direction of photo-realism, and of course the swinging is not done.

An antifoundationalist will say that what is true of the realm of art—settled conventions can always be supplanted—is true of every realm, although the ratio between periods of stability when everyone knows what's what and moments of change will differ among practices and in the history of a single practice. For some time now the bywords in politics, at least in the West, have been "autonomy," "choice," "liberty," and "equality," an ensemble of liberal values that has supplanted the value of obedience to revealed truth that had for so long informed political action. In 1992 Francis Fukuyama went so far as to announce the "end of history," the end, that is, of arguments about what normative principles should guide the political actions of states. We have reached, he said, "the end point of ideological evolution and the universalization of Western liberal democracy as the final form of government" (*The End of History and the Last Man*). History, however, has turned out to be less teleological—that is, moving in the direction of a final perfected state of things—than episodic, with Western liberal democracy temporarily in the ascendency, at least in departments of philosophy and political science, but facing a strong challenge from a resurgent nationalism and an ever-growing number of fiercely theocratic regimes. Fifty years from now, who knows?

None of this will be surprising to the antifoundationalist, who looks not to gods or invariant first principles for an understanding of how the world works, but to the protean capacity of man to make and remake the environment (political, economic, artistic, cultural, domestic) in which he thinks and acts. Antifoundationalism is a theoretical version of the very old maxim attributed to the sophist Protagoras, "Man is the measure of all things."

If that is the case, if the "right way" is neither revealed in a scripture, nor waiting for us at the end of nature's unfolding design, but is something men and women endlessly fashion and refashion, then argument is absent from no area of human life, even science. Argument, in short, occupies the whole of the antifoundationalist world and therefore the skill of arguing is not secondary but primary. From a foundationalist perspective, argument is both secondary and suspect because it focuses not on what is true, but on what is probable, not on what can be proven (in the mathematical sense), but on what can be rendered persuasive. In a foundationalist world, every significant question has a single right answer and the task is to arrive at it, at which point argument becomes what I have called elsewhere a "self-consuming artifact"; as Perelman and Olbrechts-Tyteca observe, success in the foundationalist project "means progressively reducing resort to argumentation up until the moment when its use becomes entirely superfluous." In an antifoundationalist world, in contrast, every significant question has many plausible answers and there is no algorithm or master narrative that directs us to the absolutely correct one. What stands in place of the absent algorithm or master narrative are the arts of persuasion, the arts by which an orator or a statesman or a legislator or a judge gets his hearers to accept as true what he believes to be true.

Foundationalists complain that the trouble with persuasion is that it is contingent: its outcomes are not calculable but depend on many shifting and unpredictable factors; its successes are temporary and provisional rather than final and definitive; its effects may take for centuries or they may last only for a moment or a week or a year. But this deficiency of argument—it begins and ends in probabilities and never achieves bedrock, absolute certainty—is in fact a deficiency only if there is a surer method for determining what is true and right than the back-and-forth dialectic of competing probabilities, and the lesson of antifoundationalism is that there isn't one. And if truths and correct policies are not "out there," waiting to be discovered by the clear-eyed bias-free observer, but are established in the course of disputation, the skills of disputation—the arts of rhetoric or argument—are the skills by means of which political orders and indeed civilizations are built.

The Declaration of Independence

In order to see how this is done, we need only look at our own Declaration of Independence, the inaugurating document of our democracy. The Declaration is an example of what is called a declarative or performative speech act, a speech act that brings into being the entity to which it refers. (The term was introduced by J. L. Austin in his *How to Do Things with Words*, 1962.) The classic example is the marriage ceremony that concludes with the uttering of a few words, "I now pronounce you husband and wife" (now that we have gay marriage, the formula varies). Simply by virtue of those words something new—a couple—has come into the world that did not exist before. The naming of the thing is simultaneously the making of it. Of course, it's not that simple. Not just anyone can say "I now pronounce you husband and wife" and have it stick. You have to be an accredited person—a minister, a judge, a town clerk, a ship's captain—and you have to have some government authorization before you can issue a certificate with legal standing. Declarative speech acts—speech acts that create the objects they point to—are typically embedded in a network of agencies, rules, formal procedures, and systems of verification that confer on them authority and force.

But what if there is no such network, or what if the whole point of the declarative speech act is to cut loose from the existing network, to declare independence of it? What authorizes that kind of speech act? The answer is "nothing." That kind of speech act authorizes itself and is finally indistinguishable from an act of force, a breaking away from existing structures that is, strictly speaking, illegitimate, because the norms that have previously conferred legitimacy are, at this very instant, being renounced and abandoned. For the moment of the breaking away there is no ground on which the agent claiming agency can stand, but by the time the declarative utterance completes itself, a new ground has been established, pretty much out of thin air.

That is the structure of the Declaration of Independence: we hereby declare that we are independent of England and we mark that independence by signing our names. But as Jacques Derrida points out in his essay "Declarations of Independence" (1976), "there was no signer, *by right*, before the Declaration which itself remains the producer and guarantor of its own signature." The signers of the Declaration could have been anybody, could have been fifty-six men picked off the street. Documents are usually authoritative only if the "right" person signs (as marriages are official only if the certificate is signed by someone authorized to do so), but the signer of the Declaration is the "right" person to do so simply by virtue of his signature—he declares his own fitness for the job—and not by virtue of a status he possessed beforehand. "The signature invents the signer."

Derrida poses the key question: "whether independence is stated or produced by this utterance. . . . Is it that the good people have already freed themselves in fact and are only stating the fact of this emancipation in the Declaration? Or is it rather that they free themselves at the instant of, and by, the signature of this Declaration?" In Derrida's view, the second answer is obviously the right one. Although the Declaration is made in the name of "we the people," the people, he says, "do *not* exist as an entity . . . *before* this declaration." The entity, the people, "gives birth to itself." It is a grand instance of a spin that sticks.

Once the initial declaration has taken—once a new order is declared into being—additional documentary bricks build up the structure: a constitution, a system of courts in the business of creating endless pieces of paper, a system of accredited colleges and universities issuing more pieces of paper in the form of diplomas, administrative agencies that issue still more pieces of paper, a currency (also paper), state and municipal governments that are their own printing presses, tax assessors, tax collectors, deeds, leases, foreclosure mechanisms, bankruptcy procedures, telephone records, bank records, rating agencies, visas, passports, marriage certificates, licenses for the practice of just about anything, and much more. And lo and behold, before you know it, an entire world is in place underwritten by writings, each of which rests finally on the doubtful foundation of a declaration of independence or some other self-authorizing act of political force.

When the poet Andrew Marvell celebrates Oliver Cromwell's rise to power, he makes the birth of Cromwell's legitimacy coincide with the death of the king whose head he has cut off. (Not literally, of course; Cromwell was not the executioner.) "This was the memorable hour / Which first assured the forced power" ("An Horation Ode upon Cromwell's Return from Ireland," 1650). The power is assured—given authority and durability—by its own exercise. Cromwell's accomplishment is to "ruin the great work of time"—the line of British monarchy—"And cast the kingdom old / Into another mould." That is, by sheer force of will he alters the form of government, and in doing so, Marvell notes, he repeats an earlier act of usurpation: "So when they did design / The Capitol's first line, / A bleeding head, where they begun / Did fright the architects to run." The "first" establishment of a regime is not really the first; preceding it is an earlier originary act of violence, and although the memory of that act may be lost or erased from current histories, it is always possible to "unearth" it and realize once again that there never can be a "clean" inauguration of a state, an inauguration that is innocent of illegitimate force. There is always a bleeding head (and beneath that, another), no matter how many pieces of paper have been piled on top of it in an effort to erase it from history. Moreover, as Marvell reminds us in the poem's closing lines, a state founded by a declaration without ground can maintain itself only by endlessly shoring up its nonfoundation: "The same arts that did gain / A power, must it maintain." A declarative argument's work is never really as definitive as its utterer hopes; sooner or later the work will have to be done all over again, lest the structure fall back into the abyss from which it came.

The never-ending process by which worlds are constituted and maintained by words has been called "constitutive rhetoric." Constitutive rhetoric, Maurice Charland explains, "simultaneously presumes and asserts a fundamental collective identity, offers a narrative that demonstrates that identity, and issues a call to affirm that identity" (*Encyclopedia of Rhetoric*, 2001). It is usually assumed that the audience of a rhetorical performance has its own shape to which the orator or polemicist must be responsive, but Charland is saying (along with Kenneth Burke and others) that the powerful rhetorician creates the audience he is addressing, talking it into being even as he claims to be deferring to its independence: "members of an audience are brought to share a common identity with each other or a speaker." Once that common identity has been forged, a community exists, and it can be urged to collective action. "Constitutive rhetoric constructs political subjects through effects of identification that (1) provide a collective identity for an addressed audience; (2) construct the audience as a subject in history; and (3) demand that subjects act in accordance with their identity as enacted in history." (Mark

Antony's speech in *Julius Caesar* is a perfect example, as are, alas, the speeches of Hitler.) Such constituted subjects will know what is true and relevant, recognize what is authoritative, have a clear sense of the paths of error, and feel an obligation to do the right thing, where "true," "relevant," "authoritative," "error," and the "right thing" all have the content given to them by the constitutive act of community-making.

In this vision (which comes down to us from the sophists Gorgias and Protagoras) the "constitutive power of utterances" is wide ranging; for in the absence of foundational truths, values, and ethical obligations, something must supply a simulacrum of the essences that elude our epistemological grasp, and that something is discourse—speech, rhetoric, argument—which, says Charland, is "productive of the very categories by which the world, and indeed the self, are understood." Rhetoric and argument, rather than being servants of an antecedent reality, are the fashioners of that reality. Rhetoric, in short (and this is the large claim), is "fundamentally ontological," concerned not just with cosmetically burnishing the surface of things (the role traditionally assigned to the artful use of words), but with constituting them. Rhetoric, Charland concludes, is in the business of "establishing the very foundations of the political life-world." Insofar as there are foundations, they are put in place by the very arts foundationalists scorn as ephemeral and seductive, the arts of persuasion and argument. It is time to repeat a statement made at the beginning of this book, a statement whose force we are now in a better position to appreciate: Arguments about the world come first, the world comes second. Words make the world.

CHAPTER 3

DOMESTIC ARGUMENTS

◆————————◆

He Says, She Says:
The First Domestic Quarrel

OF THE WORLDS words make, the one closest and most familiar to us is marriage (shorthand for any domestic partnership). The relationship between marriage and the art of language is, to put it mildly, complex. A marriage between two persons who have taken a vow of silence (extending to the use of sign language and written notes) presents obvious problems. How would breaches be acknowledged and repaired? A marriage where one person speaks and the other remains silent is equally problematic. How is compatibility to be established and maintained? A marriage where both partners speak but never bring up the issues that trouble them on a deep level will go forward, but at what level of satisfaction? The river may run smooth but shallow. A marriage where resentments, recriminations, accusations, and criticism are aired daily will be arresting as a piece of drama (or farce), but will it be livable?

I grew up inside that last kind of marriage. Never a dull moment. A friend who lived next door said that he didn't need to turn on the TV to be entertained; all he had to do was open the window and listen to us. My wife, an only child, had the opposite experience. In her house, she never heard an argument or even a raised voice. The universe she lived in was without conflict (as far as she could tell), which made it difficult for her when later on conflict entered her life, as it always will. Even now a good shouting match seems to me like a clearing of the throat; she receives it as an assault. A large part of the adjustment each of us has to make involves the management of words. Too few and a connection seems broken; too many and the ruptures seem to multiply. How does anyone ever get this right?

John Milton asks that question when in *Paradise Lost*, book 9, he imagines (it is not in Genesis) what the first-ever domestic quarrel was like. Adam and Eve are discussing how best to perform the work they have been assigned, the work of tending the Garden of Eden. Eve comes up with a plan that would, she thinks, increase their efficiency: let's work separately, for if we work together "looks intervene and smiles" interrupt "our day's work brought to little" and "the hour of supper comes unearned" (222–25). Adam responds well by first thanking Eve for her thoughts—"Well hast thou motioned, well thy thoughts employed" (229)—and then reminds her that God is not a timekeeping taskmaster but a benevolent father who wants them to enjoy his bounty: "Yet not so strictly hath our Lord imposed / Labor, as to debar us when we need / Refreshment, whether food or talk between" (235–37).

So far, so good. But then, out of the blue, Adam says something that puts an entirely new spin on the situation: "but if much converse perhaps / Thee satiate, to short absence I could yield" (247–48). For no reason at all, Adam hears Eve's concern that displays of affection might interfere with their task as a rejection: he is saying, "Well, if you're tired of me, I'll agree to a short separation." But she has neither said nor thought anything of the kind. Adam's characterization of the possible (and hidden) motive for her suggested plan comes (if it comes from anywhere) from his own insecurity; there is in him a lack of self-esteem that leads to thinking of himself as a person someone else might easily get tired of, and in the course of his conceiving himself as that kind of person, he conceives Eve as the kind of person who would quickly (they've been in Eden for only a few days) become tired of a partner.

This leads me to pronounce the first, and most important, rule of domestic quarrels: *They are performances of personality creation, and the personalities they create form quickly and tend to stick around for a long time.* Each partner peoples the stage of the relationship with the theatrical (but increasingly real) characters generated by his or her point of view: Adam's playbook reads, she's the fickle type; I'm the sensitive type, but I'm also reasonable and willing to indulge her ("to short absence I could yield").

At this point Eve, like every other domestic partner, has

a choice of how to respond. She can take the high road and not rise to the bait. Or, recognizing Adam's anxiety, she can allay it and say something like, "No, of course I am not tired of you; in fact, my affection for you is so strong that it gets in the way of our work. But if you don't like my suggestion, I'll be happy to listen to yours." That is, she can play the role so many of her daughters will be called on to play, the soother of a male's bruised—actually self-bruised—ego. Instead she responds to Adam's words in kind, "As one who loves, and some unkindness meets" (271). That's the role she will play; she will match Adam's hurt feelings with her own and thereby join him in a cycle of ever-spiraling recriminations.

In addition to suggesting that she might be tired of him, Adam has reminded Eve that a "malicious foe" is out there plotting against them, and he declares that they will be better able to resist him if they stay together, "where each / To other speedy aid might lend at need" (259–60). Just as Adam has interpreted her proposal to work separately as a sign that she prefers to be apart from him, so Eve now interprets Adam's worry about the foe stalking them as a lack of faith in her ability to withstand an assault on her own. Oh, I get it: I'm just a weak little woman who is helpless unless her man is at her side! How could you think of me that way? "Thoughts, which how found they harbor in thy breast / Adam misthought of her to thee so dear" (288–89). Eve wonders where Adam's thoughts about her have come from and how they have so quickly occupied a prominent place in his heart. She is being "misthought," that is, wrought by his negative thoughts into a form not really hers; and she returns the (dis)favor by thinking of him as unkind and ungenerous. She is saying, "I didn't think that you were the kind of person who would think that I was the kind of person implied by your thoughts." The sequence is one we all recognize from our own experience: the aggrieved party asks, "What kind of person do you think I am?" and the other aggrieved party replies, "What kind of person do you think *I* am?" Together they are making themselves into the kinds of people they will be at the end of the altercation, unless something intervenes to change their increasingly unhappy course.

What began as a cooperative discussion of gardening strategies has turned into a jockeying for power, and the jockeying picks up in intensity after Eve eats the forbidden apple and Adam joins her in the act of primal disobedience. After the first bout of post-Edenic sex, they fall asleep and awake with a rueful awareness of what they have done. Immediately Adam says, if only you had "hearkened to my words" when that "strange / Desire of wandering . . . possessed thee" (1134, 1135–36), we would still be happy. Eve, "moved with touch of blame," cannot believe what she is hearing and reminds him that the result might well have been the same had they stayed together, and besides, what is she supposed to do, never stray from his side and be "a lifeless rib" (1154)?

And then she delivers the zinger. I thought you were the head of the household; why didn't you just "Command me absolutely not to go" (1156)? Adam explodes, "ingrateful Eve" (1164), I gave up everything for you by joining in your crime and "willingly chose . . . death with thee" (1167). And then he voices a generalization men will repeat through the ages: if a man lets a woman have her way and something goes wrong, "She first his weak indulgence will accuse" (1186). Book 9 ends with a three-line description of every domestic quarrel that follows the template of this one, that is, of every domestic quarrel: "Thus they in mutual accusation spent / The fruitless hours, but neither self-condemning, / And of their vain contest appeared no end" (1187–89).

The Marriage Manuals

It is a remarkable scene that in its two-hundred-plus lines rings every change rehearsed by the self-help marriage books that seem to come out daily. These books fall into two parts: the diagnostic part and the recommendation, or way-out-of-the-impasse, part. Typically the diagnosis is developed through the unpacking of examples involving embattled couples (like Adam and Eve) who have moved from the easy intimacy characterizing the first flush of romantic love to an unhappy marital battlefield characterized by anger, blame, aggression, self-extenuation, recriminations, frustrations, infidelity, silence, withdrawal, sense of injured merit, and, above all, loss of connection. The first task is to understand "how we got here" and the second, much more difficult, is to figure out how to get the connection back. Trying to understand "how we got here" harbors its own dangers, for there is a temptation to think that the quarrel had a punctual beginning—as if a bell had rung announcing "now we quarrel"—which is also the temptation to trace the origin of the quarrel back to something your partner said or to your partner's too hasty interpretation of something you said. Not only is this a disastrous strategy (because it only reignites the quarrel it was meant to tamp down), it is a misreading of the career of a domestic argument, which does not so much unfold as erupt against a background of what at least one of the participants regards as a companionable conversation. Adam doesn't have the slightest idea that what he has said in response to Eve's suggestion that they work separately has been received by her as a criticism. He is behind the eight ball before he knows that there is something wrong.

This leads me to pronounce the second rule of domestic arguments: *They do not have a formal beginning, and by the time you know you're in one, it's too late.* Of course, some arguments do have formal beginnings, but that is because they are exercises—think of debating societies or moot-court competitions—and the participants are invested in the positions they take only for the duration of the exercise. If you're proceeding in this spirit, and you say to someone, "Let's argue," and your interlocutor replies "About what?" you might reply, "About anything at all; I just want to practice." (As does the lead character in the Monty Python sketch.)

Domestic arguments aren't like that. The participants aren't looking to have an argument (some spouses might disagree), but stumble into it and then make it bigger and bigger by trying to undo its effects. Domestic arguments resemble the fabled hydra: every time one party makes what he or she thinks to be a telling point and cuts off a main strain or head of the other's position, two grow in its place. Even the attempt to exit from a domestic argument ("I've had enough of this") only renews it: It's easy to fall into a quarrel but almost impossible to get out of one.

In their book *How to Improve Your Marriage Without Talking About It* (2007), Patricia Love and Steven Stosny offer a composite of a conversation they have heard a thousand times:

SHE: You're *never* home. If you think I'm going to warm up your dinner, forget it. I am not your maid.

HE: I came home in time two days this week. You *know* how much work we have.

SHE: Oh, two days out of five. I guess I should consider myself lucky. I really wanted to get married to have a husband forty percent of the time.

HE: Why should I bother to come home when I have to put up with *this*!

She begins in full aggressive mode, but by pushing so hard she leaves herself vulnerable on the flank. First she makes a categorical statement—"You're *never* home"—that invites a factual correction—"two days out of five"; then she imputes to him a demand he hasn't made—"If you think . . ."—and refuses to meet it; and finally she ratchets up the stakes by implying that the present moment is just one more instance of his assuming that she is there to serve him. (This is her version of "lifeless rib.") In turn he reminds her that he is the one who brings home the bacon—"You *know* how much work we have" (as opposed to how much work she doesn't have)—and therefore should not be criticized for all he does on her behalf. But she comes back strong, turning his numerical correction into a self-accusation—you admit that you're here only 40 percent of the time—and pretty much saying that this is not the train she bought a ticket for; only slightly below the surface is a question: What am I doing here anyway? He is ready with his own version of that question: Why should I keep coming home when all I get is this kind of grief?

Love and Stosny echo Milton (unintentionally, I presume) when they remark, "They could go on all night—and sometimes they have—going back and forth in vain attempts to decide who was right." The attempt is vain both because in this kind of argument no one is right, and because the desire to be right is what produces the impasse and ensures that closure will never occur. The impasse is also produced by the asymmetry of the two parties' experience. Like their fellow marriage counselors, Love and Stosny explain the difficulties couples get into by identifying the different sensitivities that lead men and women to react as they do. Women, they say, operate out of a fear that they will be isolated, abandoned, and rendered invisible; men react badly, and with shame, in the face of any suggestion that they are poor providers, inadequate protectors, weak, and wrong. In the little dialogue analyzed above the wife is saying, "You've abandoned me," and the husband is saying, "Why are you criticizing me for doing what I'm supposed to do; aren't I doing enough?" (One might object that this scene is filled with challengeable stereotypes; by and large the marriage manuals assume a traditional couple occupying traditional roles.)

What each experiences as anxiety—I will be left alone; I will be regarded as a failure—is experienced by the other as criticism and blame. In fact, both are lamenting a loss of connection and trying to recover it by means that are, to say the least, counterproductive. Like many couples in similar situations, "they are both feeling devalued by the other, even though no one is trying to devalue anybody" (Love and Stosny). Situated as they are in the midst of their contrasting anxieties, men and women simply can't hear each other; each reacts as if what is being said by the other was being said by herself or himself; the scene unfolds for each as if he or she were both speaker and receiver; the other's perspective is edited out or eclipsed by the strength of the perspective in which one habitually lives. Men don't understand women's fear of isolation because "they don't know what it feels like" (Love and Stosny); and women don't understand men's deep anxiety about being publicly shamed because they don't know what it feels like. (Think of all those movie Westerns in which a woman urges her man to walk away from a fight or just leave town only to hear him say that if he did that he couldn't live with himself.)

This leads me to the third rule of domestic quarrels: *They are never about their surface content (who's going to walk the dog tonight?), but about the asymmetrical needs each party is intent on satisfying in ways that act as negative triggers for the other*: "she wants him to prove that he loves her so that she can feel connected and thereby reduce her fear of isolation or privation. But the fact that she wants him to *prove* that he loves her makes him feel like a failure—if he were a good husband, he wouldn't have to prove it" (Love and Stosny). A misplaced focus on who is factually right means that neither will get what he or she wants because the underlying anxieties, rather than being helpfully addressed, are exacerbated: "*When a woman shames a man, she's wrong even if she's right. When a man stimulates a woman's fear, he is wrong even if he's right*" (Love and Stosny).

Another brief dialogue presented by Love and Stosny illustrates the point:

SHEILA: It's cold in here.

RANDY: How can you say that? It's seventy degrees.

Sheila is saying "I *feel* cold," a statement about what she is experiencing, not about the temperature. Randy hears it as a factual error, and, more important, as a criticism of his performance: were he a better husband, his wife would be comfortable. This isn't going to go well.

In fact, it will never go well. John M. Gottman and Nan Silver draw the bleak conclusion, a conclusion that will come as no surprise to readers of this book: "*Most marital arguments cannot be resolved. Couples spend year after year trying to change each other's mind—but it can't be done. This is because most of their disagreements are rooted in fundamental differences of lifestyle, personality, or values*" (*The Seven Principles for Making Marriage Work*, 1999). Earlier I pointed out that most political arguments cannot be resolved (or won), for pretty much the same reason: whatever the local content of the argument, its true content is the opposition between global points of view so deeply embedded that they are for the most part inaccessible; and even if it were possible to access them (after a lot of hard work) their force would not be much diminished because they ground the very identity of those committed to them. In this respect political arguments and marital arguments are the same, except for one important difference: if you find yourself in an intractable political argument, you can extricate yourself and go home, but it will be the intractable domestic argument that you go home to; it's always waiting for you.

The Comedy of Marriage

Because almost everyone comes home to marital trouble, it has long been a staple theme of literature, especially of comedy. The genre goes back at least as far as Homer's *Odyssey*, where Penelope—a wife who can justly complain that her husband is never home—wards off 108 suitors for two decades, devising dodges and excuses that would be the envy of any sitcom writer while waiting for the husband who expects her to remain chaste and faithful during his twenty-year night out with the boys.

Shakespeare is less the dramatist of marriage than of the premarriage courting dance that is displayed and probed in plays such as *The Taming of the Shrew*, *As You Like It*, *Twelfth Night*, and *Much Ado About Nothing*. In these plays (and also more darkly in *Antony and Cleopatra*, *Troilus and Cressida*, *Measure for Measure*, *The Winter's Tale*, and *Othello*) the "battle of the sexes" is presented as a battle of wits, as men and women (and sometimes men disguised as women and women as men) indulge in wordplay, one-upmanship, and "palpable hits."

The contest of wit between men and women is the entire content of Restoration comedy, with its fast-moving panorama of courtly intrigue, secret identities, marital infidelity, cuckoldry, clandestine romance, and ribald conversation. The song that opens John Dryden's *Marriage à la Mode* (1672) conveys the spirit of the genre perfectly: "Why should a foolish marriage vow / Which long ago was made / Oblige us to each other now / When passion is decayed? / We loved, and we loved as long as we could / 'Til our love was loved out in us both / But our marriage is dead, when the pleasure is fled: / T'was pleasure that made it an oath." The question of what does and does not bind us together in a marriage or an extended relationship is explored again and again by novelists from Samuel Richardson to Jane Austen to George Eliot to John Updike (to mention but a very few), and by lyricists like Catullus, Ovid, Petrarch, Shakespeare, Donne, Keats, Browning, Auden, and Adrienne Rich (again a severely truncated list).

In the twentieth century, the apparently interminable and inexhaustible meditation on marriage is transferred to the screen in films like *Adam's Rib*, *Woman of the Year*, *The Philadelphia Story*, *The Awful Truth*, *Marriage Is a Private Affair*, *The Best Years of Our Lives*, the Thin Man series, *Scenes from a Marriage*, *The Four Poster*, a bunch of Doris Day comedies, *Kramer vs. Kramer*, *Hannah and Her Sisters*, and *Two for the Road*. Perhaps the most caustic literary (and filmic) representation of marriage and its discontents is Edward Albee's *Who's Afraid of Virginia Woolf?* (1962), a very long play in which a young couple unwisely accept an invitation to drop in at the home of an aggressively dysfunctional couple, George and Martha, and find themselves first spectators of, and then participants in, an almost athletic exchange of barbs and savage put-downs that at once threatens the older couple's marriage and is the glue that holds it together, if anything does. (George says almost admiringly, "Martha's a devil with language.")

Basing a marriage on a ritual of escalating insults is a risky business, and one never knows when watching *Who's Afraid of Virginia Woolf?* whether, as both Martha and George predict, one more word will detonate the marital atomic bomb and blow the whole thing up. The tension that crackles on the stage is felt by the viewer, who, like the characters, never relaxes. This is not the case, however, with the radio and TV versions of the trope, which differ from the Albee drama in not taking the verbal sparring seriously, and instead regard it as spectacle and play. The purest example is perhaps *The Bickersons*, a 1946–1951 radio spot of five to fifteen minutes, starring Frances Langford and Don Ameche as Blanche and John Bickerson. Bicker is what they do, bicker is who they are. Typically an episode will begin with John's loud snoring—Blanche says it's "like sleeping with an outboard motor"—and John's denial upon being awakened that he is snoring at all. "You're snoring, I don't snore, yes you do, no I don't." That is the level of exchange in what is basically a series of one-liners:

BLANCHE: You don't know the meaning of the word "matrimony."

JOHN: It's not a word but a sentence.

BLANCHE: It wouldn't hurt to kiss me good night.

JOHN: It hurts.

This could, and does, go on forever, and the tenor, despite the content of what is being said, is level, and even, in a curious way, calm. The mode here is performance, and the performance is of wit (not of a very high order), with each partner experiencing the satisfaction of being able to produce a comeback. One doesn't worry about the state of the Bickersons' marriage, which is not threatened but sustained in its narrow range by the activity both husband and wife relish.

This is true also of the much later *Married . . . with Children* (1987–1997), a Fox sitcom about a proudly dysfunctional family of four—Al and Peg Bundy and their children, Kelly and Bud—none of whom has a redeeming feature. They are alternately loud, crude, cruel, insensitive, bombastic, scheming, boastful, duplicitous, lecherous, and greedy. Each of them delights in saying the most terrible things about the others, but no one takes offense for more than a merely theatrical half-second: the wall-to-wall marital static that surrounds them is just the medium in which they live; they wouldn't know what to do without it. In one scene, Peg asks Al, "What's that song you hate?" and as she sings it to him, Al is cutting his toenails with his foot almost in her face. In another, she complains, "You don't find me attractive anymore," to which he replies "So?" The spirit of the program is captured in a pronouncement by Al: "Even if you were beautiful like that girl on TV, I'd still ignore you because you're my wife." That is, don't you know what marriage is about? Don't you know that husbands are always turned off by their wives and spend every minute of the day regretting they got married at all? (One of Dryden's characters in *Marriage à la Mode* makes the same point: when a friend says to him, "You dislike her for no other reason but because she's your wife," he replies, "And is that not enough?")

The creators of the program resisted network pressure to leaven the loaf with physical affection: "no hugs" was the rule; no "cuddly" endings. The point, the producers explained, was to have a program you could watch without worrying that "you're going to learn a lesson," like love conquers all. The intention was to make viewers feel good by immersing them in a marriage worse than their own. When he was pitching the program to local outlets, cocreator Michael Moye eschewed the usual lengthy promo and asked those assembled, "How many of you are married?" When a large number of hands went up, he posed a follow-up: "Still having sex?" Forests of hands went down. He then put a third question: "And your kids? Turned out as you hoped they would?" In a few seconds he had conveyed to the members of his audience exactly what the program would be like—a succession of scenes in which every bad aspect of their own matrimonial experience would be at once caricatured and validated; after all, if everyone is in the same boat, the fact that you're in it can't be so bad. Like the Bickersons, the Bundys are held together, not pulled apart, by the verbal bombs they lob at one another. And when a threat from the outside is perceived they stick together in their fashion, defending what Al calls "the Bundy honor," which is not honor among thieves, but honor among marital misanthropes.

The Bickersons and the Bundys occupy the far end of the spectrum of representations of marriage in popular media. At the other end are shows such as *Ozzie and Harriet*, *Father Knows Best*, *The Dick Van Dyke Show*, *The Partridge Family*, *The Brady Bunch*, and *I Love Lucy*. In a sense, these shows are about nothing. But they are not about nothing in the way *Seinfeld* is about nothing: they don't delight in illustrating again and again how the most insignificant difference—say between those who hang toilet paper in an overhand style and those who prefer the underhand position—can lead to a heated discussion involving finer and finer distinctions. No, these relentlessly benign shows are *really* about nothing. In *Ozzie and Harriet* the discussion, never heated, will be about whether Ricky is going to a dance or whether Ozzie can talk Harriet into allowing him to buy a pool table for the now-empty boys' room. (This is the big, and only question, of the series' last episode.) In *The Dick Van Dyke Show* something that looks like a real issue will occasionally emerge—should Laura (Mary Tyler Moore) open Rob's mail because, after all, he's going to tell her what's in the letter anyway?—but the question is only a pretext for an episode-long riff on the inability of women to stifle their curiosity. In the final scene, Laura, unable to stop herself, opens a package containing an inflatable boat; the boat inflates; she tries to hide it and is still trying when Rob comes home from his job as a comedy writer. They laugh and make up. Any marital tension in this show (there is hardly any in *Ozzie and Harriet*) is short-lived, superficial, and occurs against a backdrop of an unquestioned deep affection that surrounds and cushions altercations that are typically the result either of comical misunderstandings or of well-intentioned plans gone awry.

Deep affection also characterizes the relationship between Lucy (Lucille Ball) and her husband, Ricky (Desi Arnaz). The plot usually turns on the schemes Lucy and her sidekick, Ethel (Vivian Vance), think up in an effort to gain a measure of independence from their husbands. The effort always fails, but in the meantime Ball has many opportunities to show off her skills as a physical, sight-gag comedienne. Lucy and Ricky trade mild complaints about her spending, his accent, a new piece of furniture, a new hat, taking a vacation. Exasperation is continually expressed but it is barely skin-deep; the true spirit of the show is captured by its theme song: "I love Lucy and she loves me / We're as happy as two can be. / Sometimes we quarrel but then / How we love making up again."

The insults and one-liners cut a bit deeper, but finally not all that deep, in *All in the Family* (1971–1979), which has a political edge other sitcoms about marriage avoid. When watching *All in the Family*, you're in danger of learning a lesson, usually about tolerance or antidiscrimination. Archie Bunker (Carroll O'Connor) is a lower-middle-class good-hearted bigot. He and his liberal son-in-law (played by Rob Reiner) are constantly at odds, arguing about President Nixon, feminism, smoking, African Americans—everything. He calls his daughter (Sally Struthers) "little girl," even though she's a married woman, he calls his wife (Jean Stapleton) "dingbat," rolls his eyes at her naïveté, and orders her around as if she were a servant, and she responds with good-natured forbearance and unfailing love. It is reciprocated. The not-so-secret secret is that Archie's bombast is defensive—he is afraid both of feelings and of the modern world, where the lines of social demarcation he has long taken for granted are blurring—and that underneath it all he is a man seeking reassurance from those who sustain him, despite the acerbic words he sends their way, more or less reflexively. Once again the song that opens every episode tells the story. "Those were the days," Edith and Archie sing in a tribute both to the past they remember nostalgically and the present they occupy quite happily, despite the appearance of conflict.

The same combination of surface conflict and abiding affection undergirds another classic working-class sitcom— *The Honeymooners* (1955–1956). Like Archie Bunker, Ralph Kramden (Jackie Gleason) is an overweight blowhard who still harbors dreams of the wealth and success he hasn't achieved and will never achieve. He and his dim-witted buddy and neighbor, Ed Norton (Art Carney), are always coming up with crackpot ideas for striking it rich. They always fail, as Ralph's wife, Alice (Audrey Meadows), predicts they will, and she is not afraid to say "I told you so" in the course of making still another joke about her husband's weight. It is then that Ralph raises his fist and declaims, "You're going to get yours," or "You're going to the moon, Alice." The fist never lands (nor do we fear that it will), the nasty words don't really wound. At the end of one episode in which Ralph has once again humiliated himself, this time because he is jealous with no reason, he is contrite and uncharacteristically self-aware: "You were right, you're always right . . . I don't think that anyone's got a better wife. . . . I scream, yell, the slightest thing makes me jealous." That's the truth of it. Ralph loves Alice, Alice loves Ralph. In the midst of squabbling, perpetually hard times, and an endless series of comic misadventures, they remain forever the honeymooners.

Don't Argue, Just Listen

There's more to be said, both about classic shows like *Blondie and Dagwood* and *The Life of Reilly*, and more recent entries like *Married* and *Marry Me*, but the point I have been making holds: in radio and TV representations of marriage, argument is ubiquitous, but it is not serious (it's like wallpaper); it doesn't say anything about marriage in general or the marriages of the characters in particular. It's basically low verbal theater (hardly a surprise given the venue), the performance of insult rather than an exploration of its sources or effects. Because argument is not taken seriously in the sitcoms, neither the characters nor the viewers ever learn anything about how to negotiate argument or how to extricate themselves from its labyrinths or how to recover from its damage. That is what the marriage manuals promise to do and, although they vary in their diagnoses and in the approaches they recommend, they deliver a single message: arguing in marriage is a mug's game; no good can ever come of it and it would be better if it never occurred. Accordingly, what the books teach is how to avoid argument or, more precisely, how to engage in conversations from which the chief characteristics of argument—conflict, tension, anger, blame, aggressive self-assertion, complaint, criticism, and judgment—have been removed.

In a way, what has to be removed if a broken connection is to be restored are words themselves. The hurts experienced in a domestic quarrel are produced by words (and sometimes silences), and it is natural to believe that because the damage has been done by words, it can be repaired by more words. This belief is in tune with Justice Louis Brandeis's insistence that the remedy for bad speech is more speech (*Whitney v. California*, 1927), but while this may be true of political argument in the public sphere (and I don't think it is true even there), it is a disastrous recipe for marital argument because the "more" or additional words that are uttered by either partner, rather than salving wounds, almost always open new ones.

This leads me to pronounce the fourth general truth about domestic arguments: *Trying to walk back the words that have precipitated a quarrel will never work*; if you say that you have been misinterpreted, you've made a new accusation; if you say that you didn't mean what your words seemed to say, you've opened up questions about your sincerity; if you offer to clarify, you're impugning your partner's ability to understand you; if you try to defend yourself, you're recommitting and compounding the original error. That is why Love and Stosny counsel that the effort to undo the damage done by words must proceed, at least at first, in a "nonverbal way": "If you try talking, you will either fumble for the right words, or, more likely, use the wrong words . . . [f]or example, you might be asking your partner to value you, but your words will most likely devalue him or her." Instead, they advise, offer physical signs of affection, like a hug, or a cup of tea, or a lit candle, or a small gift, or an offer to help. These speak volumes and do not present the opportunities to go wrong that bedevil speech.

That is, no doubt, good advice, but in any context of marital disharmony, there will always be a time when words are unavoidable (remembering again that silence talks). What do you do then? The answer given in the marriage manuals is that you engage in what is called "active listening." Active listening is the opposite of reactive listening, listening only in order to formulate your next stinging rejoinder. Active listening is empathic; the goal is to understand exactly what your partner is saying, not to counter it, or augment it, or correct it, but simply to comprehend it. Merely to attempt active listening is to put yourself in a different relation to your partner, a relation of cooperation, not opposition. Active listening is not easy—our verbal habits in the workplace and the public square militate against it—but the ability to perform it can be enhanced by certain formulaic exercises. The one most often recommended is simple paraphrasing: "Whenever your partner says something important to you, you should state in your own words what you think your partner just said" (Matthew McKay, Patrick Fanning, Kim Paleg, *Couple Skills*, 2006). That is, you should not insert anything of your own— how hard is that!—but remain faithful to what has been said to you.

But if that is the goal, the phrase "in your own words" may contain a danger, and that is why two other therapists,

Harville Hendrix and Helen LaKelly Hunt, insist in *Making Marriage Simple* (2013) that you give back the *exact* words your partner has uttered. This is not paraphrasing, but mirroring. Don't do it your way, do it his or her way. Don't edit, repeat. The partner also has a responsibility to use "I" statements—"I feel frightened and sad when you come home late"—instead of blame statements—"Why are you home late this time?" With an "I" statement you own your feelings and don't imply that they have been caused by your partner. The point is to voice and communicate the abiding anxieties that lead you to be especially vulnerable to certain stimuli. If you do this correctly and purge your words of blame, your partner will be learning something about you rather than reacting defensively to what he or she might otherwise receive as an attack. After rehearsing to your partner what he or she has said, you ask, "Did I get it?" and if you're told you did get it, then you ask, "Is there more?" That is, did I get it all, is there something I do not yet understand?

There is in fact more, for there are two additional steps: First you tell your partner that what he or she has said "makes sense," which doesn't mean that you agree with it, but that you can see from a perspective you don't necessarily share how someone might think this way. (This is called "validating.") You then extend yourself further by empathizing with the emotional vulnerability that initiated the sequence. You say something like, "Given the traumatic experience of having been left alone in the house when both your parents were late, I can imagine how you must feel when I'm late." At each stage in this process, the irritation and desire for self-justification that so naturally well up in moments of conflict are dissipated and absorbed by the formulaic nature of the exchange. Hendrix and LaKelly Hunt observe that this kind of dialogue "can feel a bit stiff and formal," but both the stiffness and the formality are necessary to achieve the desired effect—the removal from the marital conversation of everything that makes it unpredictable and dangerous.

The idea is to create a "safe space" in which each partner can speak without fear of being verbally assaulted or ambushed. That space emerges as the usually rapid back and forth of argument is deliberately slowed down by the mannered dialogue. A truly safe dialogue "isn't supposed to be quick. To discover who our partner really is . . . we have to slow down." The promised reward for slowing down is a far-reaching change: "Your fears diminish and you begin to feel connected. You get to the point where you may completely disagree with something your partner thinks or feels. But from the open, empathic place, you grow to understand it . . . more deeply. You begin to experience your relationship as wondrous and deeply fulfilling" (Hendrix and LaKelly Hunt).

To some extent the strategy is counterintuitive, especially in a culture that values spontaneity and sincerity. Isn't it the case that, especially in intimate relationships, what we say should come directly from the heart and be a direct expression of our innermost feelings? Actually, McKay, Fanning, and Paleg explain, the reverse is true: "it's quite common for people's thoughts and behavior to change first, and the feelings to change later." Rather than allowing your first emotional response to something your partner has said to dictate (without reflection) what you say in response, train yourself to take a step back from your emotions and think about their source in your characteristic fears and anxieties, and, at the same time, think about the characteristic fears and anxieties that have led your partner to produce the words that have pressed your buttons. No longer the direct participant in an exchange that unfolds instinctively—without thought—you become instead the reflective observer of your own internal landscape and, by extension, of your partner's internal landscape, too.

And when you return from this realm of reflection to the actual dialogue you and your partner are engaging in, you will feel differently both about what is going on in the conversation and about your partner, who will be seen not as an adversary who must be defeated by your next devastating quip, but as a person whose needs deserve to be understood and met no less than do yours. By thus changing your thoughts about your partner, you will change your behavior, and in the end change your reactive, defensive feelings into feelings of sympathy, compassion, and connection. If, as McKay, Fanning, and Paleg contend, "your thoughts shape the way you feel and ultimately how you act," then it is incumbent upon you not to go with your first thoughts, but to examine them critically and, if they are negative, discard them in favor of thoughts that will help, not harm, the relationship. If personality creation is what's going on in domestic arguments, there is at least the possibility that the personalities created will be benign.

Adam and Eve Get a Second Chance

Let's test the analyses and recommendations of the marriage manuals by returning to *Paradise Lost*, book 9, and imagining how Adam and Eve might have done a better job at managing their conversation. It is a conversation, you will remember, that had a good beginning. Eve comes to Adam with a suggestion for improving the yield of their daily work; he praises her initiative but then, unaccountably, he attributes to her a motive ("If you're tired of me . . .") she shows no signs of having. In the marriage manuals, this is called "mind reading" or "assumed intent": "Assumed intent is a deadly mental error. Unconfirmed beliefs about your partner's motives can make you extremely angry, hurt, or discouraged. And if they're not true, you end up making strong responses to a phantom reality that may be tragically removed from your partner's real feelings and motives" (McKay, Fanning, and Paleg). Not only that: you end up provoking strong responses from the partner who is indignant at being wrongly characterized. That is exactly what happens—Adam "misthinks" Eve and Eve, in her turn, misthinks Adam, assigning him motives darker than the one he has assigned her—but it needn't have. Adam could have listened to his negative thought and examined it before giving it voice. Had he done that and not said, "If much converse perhaps / Thee satiate," there might have been no argument. But he did say it, and an opportunity was lost.

Eve is up next, and she too could have metaphorically turned the other cheek; she could have decided to interpret his solicitude—I am worried "lest harm / Befall thee severed from me"—as an expression of paternal affection rather than as an insult to her competence. But she doesn't and she reminds him (always with a smile) of what he already knows, that the harm he is worried about cannot be inflicted by their foe because in their unfallen state they are "not capable of death or pain" (283). Therefore, she concludes triumphantly—it is the "triumph" of having caught your partner in a bad thought about you—his fear proceeds from a low estimation of her capacities: "His fraud is then thy fear, which plainly infers / Thy equal fear that my firm faith and love / Can by his fraud be shaken or seduced" (285–87).

Eve has upped the stakes and fueled the argument rather than defusing it. Adam now has more things to answer for and he replies to her accusation of his having accused her with "healing words." But, as we have seen, words do not heal and these words, predictably, only increase the height of the mountain Adam must climb. He says that while it's true that the foe cannot harm them, even the "attempt itself" would be an aspersion on their honor, and he would be less likely to make the attempt if they were together. This is a faulty argument, and Eve pounces on it; the dishonor, she explains, would attach to the tempter, not to them "who rather double honor gain / From his surmise proved false, find peace within, / Favor from heaven, our witness from the event" (332–34). In short, gotcha! You're wrong on every count, so there!

But claiming victory in a domestic quarrel is a sure sign that both partners have suffered a defeat, the defeat inherent in exchanging the sweet connection of marital harmony for the false rewards of forensic warfare. The only way to avoid the dangers of the agonistic cycle is to break it, and you break it not by making a decisive point (as both Adam and Eve think they do time and again), but by forswearing the making of points and switching to another mode of interaction altogether.

Adam and Eve are unable to do this in the course of their quarrel, and they remain unable to do it when they later look back on their disastrous choices and accuse each other of having made the fatal mistake. When Adam generalizes from the present situation to the defects women will display in any and every situation—"Thus it shall befall / Him who to worth in women overtrusting" (1182–83)—he commits the error every marriage manual warns against: he makes an "always" or "never" statement like "You're always late" or "You never empty the dishwasher." "Always" and "never" statements do several bad things: they indicate hopelessness; your partner will never change; they willfully cancel out all the times your partner's actions did not conform to a bad model; they block the path to connection. McKay, Fanning, and Paleg call "always" and "never" statements "global labels": "When they are delivered, global labels feel correct and just. They feel like proper punishment. But the outcome is a loss of trust and a loss of closeness."

Adam's global labeling is really global; it's not just that Eve displays incorrigibly bad behavior; all women who descend from her will do the same. Later, after God has come down to judge the two miscreants and the effects of the Fall manifest themselves in nature—"Beast now with beast gan war and fowl with fowl" (bk. 10, line 710)—Adam redoubles his global accusations, "But for thee / I had persisted happy" (873–74), he says to Eve as he repulses her attempt to approach him. He blames himself (really an accusation of her) only for not understanding that "all was but a show / Rather than solid virtue, all but a rib crooked by nature" (883–85). He wishes that God had found another way to propagate the species instead of creating woman, "this fair defect" (891). He predicts that no man will ever "find out fit mate, but such / As some misfortune brings him" (899–900).

When Adam's misogynist rant ends and he falls silent ("He added not"), it is Eve's turn to speak, and one might expect from her recent past performance that she would refute him point for point and insist, as she had earlier, that he is at least as much to blame for what has happened as she is. But instead she proclaims her full responsibility, apologizes for her offense, declares her love for him, embraces him, begs him not to cast her off, tells him how much she depends on him, and—this is the best thing—asks for his help, all in lines of poetry that have the feel of an aria: "Forsake me not thus, Adam, witness Heaven / What love sincere, and reverence in my heart / I bear thee, and unweeting have offended, / Unhappily deceived; thy suppliant, / I beg, and clasp thy knees; bereave me not, / Whereon I live, thy gentle looks, thy aid / Thy counsel in this uttermost distress / My only strength and stay" (914–21).

What Eve has done here—in a gesture as mysterious in its origin as Adam's invention of her being tired of him—is remove from her discourse what Gottman and Silver in *The Seven Principles for Making Marriage Work* call "The Four Horsemen of the Apocalypse—criticism, contempt, defensiveness, and stonewalling—those hallmarks of marriage-harming conflict," hallmarks Adam has just exhibited in spades. "It's just a fact," say Gottman and Silver, that "when people feel criticized, disliked, and unappreciated they are unable to change. Instead, they feel under siege and dig in to protect themselves." Eve does not dig in, although she has done so before, and we never find out why she does something else now. The manuals counsel that if a relationship is to be repaired, the right "repair attempts" must be made and the right attempt, they tell us, is one that begins with softness. The softness Eve displays here is just the ticket, but it is also remarkable given that nothing Adam has said invites it. Gottman and Silver observe that most of the time—indeed 96 percent of the time—marital exchanges "invariably end on the same note they begin." Eve gives the lie to these odds and plays against type when she simply ignores the harshness of Adam's words and returns love for contempt, appreciation for derision, solicitude for scorn, openness for defensiveness, and humility for pride. She knows instinctively what Gottman and Silver would teach us about marriage: "For a marriage to go forward happily, you need to pardon each other and give up on past resentments."

But someone has to go first and hope that just as anger breeds more anger, forgiveness and the letting go of recriminations will lead to the cessation of hostilities and the beginning of peace. And in this instance (a crucial one in our race's history) they do. Described as "immovable," Adam is nevertheless moved when he sees Eve weeping and in distress at his feet: "As one disarmed, his anger all he lost, / And . . . with peaceful words upraised her" (945–46). He immediately takes back his blaming of her and acknowledges his more than equal part in the tragedy that has befallen them. And as he bids her "rise," he voices a conclusion and a resolution that are the sum of every marriage manual ever written: "Let us no more contend nor blame / Each other, blamed enough elsewhere, but strive / In offices of love, how we may lighten / Each other's burden" (958–61). Amen!

One of the admirable things about the marriage manuals is that often their authors freely admit to making the same mistakes they classify and criticize. This candidness is at once refreshing and distressing. It is distressing because it suggests—and this is the fifth rule of domestic quarrels—that *deep knowledge of the ways of domestic argument does not insulate you from falling into the innumerable traps awaiting anyone who enters that arena.* I wish I could say that because I have studied the manuals and analyzed literary and pop culture examples of the dilemmas they probe, I have become better able to negotiate the landmines embedded in the landscape of every marriage, including mine. But—and you don't have to take my word for it, just ask my wife—when the rubber hits the road, my behavior isn't much different from the behavior of the bumbling, terminally defensive, and self-regarding boob I was before I read a word.

No surprise there, finally, because if there is any lesson in this book, it is the lesson that the hope of rationality—the hope that we can master the contingencies of our lives by assessing and cataloging the dangers we would like to avoid—is unlikely to be realized. No matter how much you know or how long you've studied, chances are that the next time you stumble into a crisis—marital or any other—you will perform no better than you did when you were eighteen years old. And if you do perform better (as I hope to do) it will not be because you have mastered an art by reading about it or theorizing it or taking a course in it, but because you've been around the track a few times and are finally beginning to get the hang of it.

CHAPTER 4

LEGAL ARGUMENTS

◆————————◆

What You Can and Cannot Say in Court

MARITAL ARGUMENTS ERUPT when a conversation goes out of control—things being said that shouldn't be said, molehills being made into mountains, irrelevancies that take over the landscape, piling on top of the present moment all the detritus of the past, raising voices to the point of vituperation and no return. Control or some kind of equilibrium can be restored only by the artificial and highly self-conscious strategies the manuals recommend—slowing things down, letting go of past injuries, renouncing blame, honestly assessing your own part in the dynamics of the relationship, speaking in measured, not angry, tones, putting yourself in your partner's shoes, performing regular acts of appreciation, et cetera. In what I earlier named a bounded-argument space these controls do not have to be imposed by will because they are built into the structure of the discursive situation. In a bounded-argument space, the things one is obliged to say and the things one is forbidden to say are known in advance, either because they are set down in a list of rules or because they are part of the tacit knowledge internalized by every competent practitioner. The categories "that's not the kind of thing we do around here" and "that's not the kind of thing we say around here" are always in force for those in the know and are likely to be mysterious to outsiders. This is certainly the case in the law.

The September 12, 2014, edition of the *New York Post* reported that the judge in a murder trial reprimanded both the prosecution and defense lawyers for openly bickering and voicing sarcastic asides. Judge Solomon (a nice name for a judge) told the attorneys, "Let's not do this in front of the jury. I said before the trial started, if you want to argue, we can argue all you want, but not in front of the jury." A layman might think that arguments directed at a jury are exactly what goes on in court, but the opposing lawyers are not supposed to be making arguments—they are supposed to be eliciting evidence.

And not any old evidence. The evidence must be admissible and admissibility is defined by rules. It must be relevant, that is, it must bear on a disputed fact in the case; no "kitchen sink" evidence wanted. It must be material, that is, related in a strong way to the proof or disconfirmation of a specific fact at issue. If the evidence is offered on a matter requiring expert knowledge, the witness offering it must be in possession of the requisite expertise. Evidence cannot be prejudicial, that is, for example, designed to elicit outrage rather than to provide the jury with material information. It cannot be misleading, that is, tending to direct the jury's attention to a tangential, legally irrelevant, matter. It must be direct, not hearsay, evidence; the witness cannot offer as evidence something he heard from someone else: "my aunt told me that she heard him say . . ." An attorney cannot elicit the same evidence over and over again. An attorney cannot elicit an opinion in the guise of eliciting evidence. An attorney cannot put evidence in a witness's mouth by asking a leading question, a question that assumes its answer, unless the witness has been designated as "hostile." If the evidence is documentary, the document on exhibit should be the original, not a copy. If the evidence offered by the government has come to light only because of information illegally obtained—by coercion or torture as in Clint Eastwood's *Dirty Harry*—it will be ruled inadmissible. If the evidence is in the possession of a witness whose name was not disclosed to the other party during the process of discovery—the equivalent of disclosing what's in your poker hand—that witness may be barred from testifying.

Each of these rules of evidence (and there are many, many more than I have listed) has its exceptions, and the conditions under which those exceptions can be invoked are spelled out in detail (although, of course, the precision of the spelling out does not preclude disagreements about application). The existence of exceptions does not make the rules less strict, but more strict: the lawyer is not liberated by the exceptions, but further constrained by them because there are more things to remember and more ways to go wrong. Indeed, constraint marks the entire process; no one can just say anything he or she thinks might contribute to the establishing of truth. Often a piece of evidence the litigator regards as dispositive—pointing to a final resolution of the dispute at hand—will be the piece of evidence that is excluded.

What makes sense of all this is the adversary nature of the legal proceeding, at least in the United States. Here is a brief account of what is usually called the "adversary system": "Adverse parties each present a self-serving version of the truth to a presumably disinterested fact finder, judge or jury, which hears the evidence each party presents and decides in a disinterested fashion what actually happened" (*Evidence: Text, Cases and Problems*, ed. Ronald Allen, Richard Kuhns, Eleanor Swift, David Schwartz, and Michael Pardo, 2011). Already this sounds strange: rather than engaging in a cooperative search for the truth, the parties put forward the versions of the truth that support the outcome they respectively prefer and wait for the trier of fact to decide between them. It's a rhetorical contest, a battle of verbal gladiators.

It didn't have to be that way: as the editors of the evidence case book I have just cited point out, the law "could permit the parties to present whatever evidence they like, [permit] the fact finders to make whatever investigation they like, and let the natural reasoning process of the fact finders lead them to whatever decision they believe to be appropriate." Why not do this? Why not let everything in and trust juries to sort it out, weighing the evidence as they do in the routines of everyday life? Why not let it unfold naturally?

The answer is that the world of the law is anything but natural; it is self-consciously artificial, an interlocking set of conventions within which ordinary words bear special meanings that are recognized with ease by insiders but will seem opaque and obfuscating to outsiders. The layperson ignorant of the law's ways may feel that he or she is entering an alien, Alice-in-Wonderland universe where meanings, arbitrarily formulated, present an insuperable (and intended) obstacle to understanding what is going on. In the first few decades of the twentieth century a movement in legal studies called "legal realism" made just that point. The conceptual vocabulary of the law, Felix Cohen, lawyer and legal realist, complained, refers not to items in the world, but to items within its own lexicon; the vocabulary (and therefore the law) is entirely self-enclosed, and as a result its terms are not truly explanatory because they never come into contact with the social realities they purport to order. "Legal concepts," he concluded, "are supernatural entities, which do not have a verifiable existence," and legal rules, rather than being "descriptions of social facts . . . are rather theorems in an independent system" ("Transcendental Nonsense and the Functional Approach," 1935). What the system is independent of is anything outside its fictional universe. If you are an inhabitant of that universe (by virtue of your law school training and years of practice) everything will make sense, although the sense will be circular and hermetic. If you are not an inhabitant, and try to apply not legal but commonsense reasoning to the facts of a case, you are likely to get it wrong.

You might, for example, think that the character of the

defendant is an important piece of evidence: "Is he or she the kind of person likely to commit this crime?" seems to be not only a reasonable but an obviously pertinent question. But it is a question that will not be asked in the course of a trial because the jury is to be protected from knowledge of the defendant's prior bad acts: "Evidence of a person's character or a character trait is not admissible to prove that on a particular occasion the person acted in accordance with the character trait" (Rule 404 of the Federal Rules of Evidence). So the defendant is known to be someone who in the past has committed a certain kind of crime and he has now been formally accused of committing just that kind of crime, but you can't argue that in committing *this* crime he would be acting in character. Neither the argument that he'd never do this kind of thing nor the argument that this is just the kind of thing he would do is to the point.

Why not? The answer is given by the California Law Revision Commission: "Character evidence . . . subtly permits the trier of fact to reward the good man and to punish the bad man because of their respective characters" rather than because of what was done or not done at a particular time. Were the argument of character heard in the courtroom, defendants might be rewarded or punished not for what they actually did on a specific occasion but for the general conduct of their lives over time. After all, "a person who is generally honest will at least occasionally be less than fully honest; a person whom we may fairly describe as having a violent character will on many occasions react to adverse situations in a peaceful manner" (*Evidence: Texts, Cases and Problems*). The goal is not to establish the character of the defendant, but to determine whether or not he or she performed this particular illegal act on this occasion, no matter what his or her character.

If this focus on the present instance were to be replaced by a study of the defendant's character, the jury would be diverted from the main *legal* issue and become mired in issues of psychology, a discipline in which the correlating of character and behavior is an appropriate form of analysis. It is not, however, an appropriate form of legal analysis. Moreover, any piece of evidence tending to prove bad character would involve the rehearsal of unattractive and even loathsome acts, a rehearsal likely to produce a negative emotional reaction that might well cloud the jurors' judgment: "a jury, on hearing about a criminal defendant's bad character, may be willing to ignore a reasonable doubt and convict a person who may not (in the juror's view) have been sufficiently punished in the past and who may commit crimes in the future" (*Evidence: Texts, Cases and Problems*). (This danger is being courted in some states by the introduction of "risk assessment" sentencing, sentencing based on a statistical determination of whether a defendant, given his psychological and sociological profile, is likely to be a repeat offender; if he is so deemed, the sentence he receives will be longer.)

Behind these reasons for disallowing evidence of character is a picture of human agency and responsibility that is peculiar to the law and would be regarded as naïve or hopelessly idealistic in other areas of life such as, for example, marriage. In that picture, discrete acts are performed by agents with no history except the very recent history that can be causally connected to the performance of this act. (On the day before the crime was committed, he bought a gun; in the weeks leading up to the assault, he made a series of threatening phone calls.) The actor so conceived is a version of the idealized, abstract citizen imagined as a thought experiment by John Rawls and other Enlightenment theorists: he or she—or more precisely "it"—is without gender, without religion, without race, without ethnicity, without social status, without economic status, and without the lifetime of choices and experiences that have made him or her or "it" unique. When we say that all persons are equal before the law, we mean not only that in court the wealth, position, sectarian beliefs, skin color, class, and family lineage of defendants don't matter, but that defendants are regarded (for legal purposes) as having none of those things and bearing none of those distinguishing marks.

The Law's Enabling Fictions

Of course this is a fiction—Felix Cohen and the other legal realists are right—but it is a fiction required by the law's resolution to be impartial; for to be impartial is to treat all equally, whether they are or not, and therefore to set aside—not take into consideration as a basis for judgment—whatever differences may actually exist. (Impartial treatment, regularly enjoined and regularly celebrated in our culture, is a very odd thing when you begin to think about it, for it erases the differences about which people most care.) It is to that fiction that questions are addressed and it is the behavior of that fiction that is being examined in a trial; not what did this white, overeducated Jewish resident of the Upper East Side do, but what did this "person"—a rational chooser whose choices are not determined by his race, his religion, his place of residence, or his class—do?

Given that it is this fiction and not a full, red-blooded person that is on trial, a lawyer cannot (or should not) make arguments that flow from or depend on the characteristics the law is ignoring or bracketing; the law cannot reason from the mere facts of ethnicity, religious affiliation, gender, and the like. This is so even in closing summations, where some, but not all, of the restrictions on a lawyer's form of presentation are relaxed. You might ratchet up the emotional tenor of your delivery (within limits, of course), but you can't argue outside the record—outside the evidence already ruled admissible; you can't present as an argument your personal opinion; you can't make an argument stemming from the defendant's failure to testify. The fictions that are in place during the main body of the trial are still in place at its close, and they are still doing the work of delimiting the arguments a lawyer can make.

The role of fictions in the law is not limited to the courtroom trial. All legal arguments unfold against a background of some authorized institutional fiction that marks out the territory and serves both to constrain and enable lines of legitimate inquiry. In the area of First Amendment law, the enabling fiction is the distinction between speech and action in the absence of which there would be no First Amendment. Imagine a First Amendment that read "Congress shall make no law abridging freedom of action." That would amount to announcing that there shall be no law, for the monitoring and regulating of action—the compiling of a list of do's and don'ts and the specification of penalties for doing what you shouldn't do—is the entirety of what the law does; if there were no restrictions on action, a man could do whatever he liked no matter what its malign effects. When the First Amendment declares that a man can *say* whatever he likes, the pronouncement makes sense only if saying isn't doing, if the production of speech is largely a matter of sending ideas into the world and carries with it none of the dangers that attend unregulated action. In short, freedom of speech makes sense only if speech is not action.

Unfortunately, it is. As I remarked earlier, the old proverb "sticks and stones can break my bones, but names will never hurt me" is false, as you can easily see by thinking back to our discussion of marriage, an institution in which almost all the action is verbal and all the damage is inflicted by words. ("Don't I have the right to say anything I like?" will not be a successful defense if offered to an aggrieved partner.) Innumerable examples of speech-produced harms could be easily instanced. One in the news a few years ago involved the Westboro Baptist Church, a militantly antigay congregation whose members show up at the funerals of young soldiers, chanting and waving banners that say things like "Thank God for Dead Soldiers" and "You're Going to Hell." (The church is not accusing the soldiers of being gay, but claiming that their deaths are God's message to a nation that has allowed homosexuality to flourish.) Imagine the grieving mothers and fathers who at the moment of interring a loved son are forced to listen and watch as the occasion is hijacked by a group spewing hate. Talk about "harm"! It is not only that harm is inflicted by what is generally called "hate speech"; the inflicting of harm is what hate speakers intend to do; they know that words can lacerate; they want their victims to feel pain, even if the pain is emotional rather than physical, although in cases of severe emotional distress that may be a distinction without a difference. As I remarked in an earlier chapter, words are weapons that can strike you to the quick.

Perhaps the most pointed attack on the speech-action distinction with respect to the doing of harm has been made by antipornography crusaders. The law professor Catharine MacKinnon has long argued that pornography is not the representation of violence against women (it is not speech)—but the performance of violence against women (it is action). "Pornography," she insists, "is what it does and not what it says," and what it does "is factually connected in many ways to a whole array of tangible human injuries," including "discrimination, sex-based coercion, force, assault, and trafficking in sexual subordination" (*New York Review of Books*, October 1993). She and her colleague Andrea Dworkin told members of Minneapolis's city council that if they did not pass an antipornography ordinance written by the two feminists, they would in effect "permit the dissemination of materials that uphold the inferior status of women . . . permit the exploitation of live women, the sadomasochistic use of live women, the binding and torture of live women."

The ordinance passed but was struck down by a court

that did not dispute MacKinnon and Dworkin's collapsing of the distinction between speech and action ("We accept the premises of this legislation") but extended it: "racial bigotry, anti-Semitism, violence on television—these and many more [forms of speech] . . . shape our culture" (*American Booksellers Ass'n. v. Hudnut*, 1985). Pornography, the court explains, is not unique among forms of speech in its tendency to produce harmful effects; all speech has the potential to do that; for if pornography "is what pornography does, so is other speech. Hitler's orations affected how . . . Germans saw Jews." But even after thus deconstructing the speech/action distinction, the court invokes it and reminds us that the United States, unlike most other Western democracies, has decided that however insidious speech may be or how lamentable its effects, it gets protection under the First Amendment. So the court rests its conclusion on the constitutionally protected status of speech after having cheerfully pointed out that the standard rationale for this protection doesn't really hold up: as its examples show, the category of speech as a form of nonaction ("it's only words") unproductive of harm has no members. The *American Booksellers* opinion is testimony to the tenacity with which courts will hold on to a fiction that enables the law's business to be done even while acknowledging that it is, in fact, a fiction.

In the operations of First Amendment jurisprudence, the enabling fiction is shored up by a number of devices and strategies. Suppose you want to sleep in a public park, but there are laws against it. What do you do? You argue that your sleeping is part and parcel of a political protest and therefore is an expression of your views: it is not action, but speech; or, more precisely, it is "symbolic action," action that bears and sends a message. This argument prevailed in lower courts but was rejected by the Supreme Court (*Clark v. Community for Creative Non-Violence*, 1984); the important point, however, is that the argument was taken seriously. Or suppose you want to protest against the policies of a merchant and you picket his shop, brandishing signs critical of his business practices; the signs are clearly a form of expression, but if you move your protest to the merchant's house and encircle it, it could be argued that your expressive behavior has crossed a line and become an incitement to violence. (The example is taken from J. S. Mill's *On Liberty*.) A court might then decide, yes, it's speech, but it's speech "brigaded with action" (*Brandenburg v. Ohio*, 1969) and therefore does not merit First Amendment protection. Or (to cite a third example), suppose there is an ordinance forbidding the burning of an American flag, but you argue that because the act of burning is expressive of the values the flag stands for it's really speech. Then you might win at the Supreme Court as Gregory Johnson did in *Texas v. Johnson* (1989), against the protests of four dissenting justices who said that flag burning is not a genuine contribution to the marketplace of ideas and is in fact not an idea at all, but is, rather, an "inarticulate grunt" and a piece of "disagreeable conduct."

The fact that these judicial determinations go back and forth, and the transformation of speech into action and vice versa sometimes takes and sometimes doesn't is evidence of the malleability of the speech/action distinction. Given a friendly court and sufficiently ingenious attorneys almost any form of speech could be characterized as action if it could be linked to the production of violence, and almost any form of action could be characterized as speech if it can be shown to have "expressive elements" (a term of art in the discussions).

In saying this I am not urging the abandonment of the First Amendment because its conceptual underpinnings do not stand up to rigorous theoretical interrogation. The fact of legal fictions, like the distinction between speech and action, is not an embarrassment to the law but a key to the way the law necessarily works. If the task of the law is to provide citizens with a clear understanding of what behaviors are allowed and what behaviors are forbidden, the task can proceed only in the context of some account of what human beings are like, what does and does not constitute harm, what penalties are appropriate, what deterrents are likely to be effective, what crimes are major or minor, what balance is to be struck between liberty and order, and a thousand other things. And given that there are innumerable possible accounts of these matters and no natural, objective, universally accepted way of deciding among them (if there were, if the rules of behavior could be directly read off the face of nature, law would be unnecessary), any account chosen to be the basis, whether articulated or implied, of a legal system will be a construct, an official fiction that, so long as it is in place (and how such fictions are replaced with new fictions is a field of study all its own), authorizes the making of some arguments and rules out the making of some others.

Doing the Crime and Shoveling the Sidewalk

Some legal commentators believe that to show that the law rests on fictions—on constructs fashioned by men and women and not on the nature of things—is to discredit it and call into question its legitimacy. Thus, for example, law professor Mark Kelman points out that in the criminal law the conclusions reached by courts derive from preliminary, prerational (not demonstrated by independent reasons to be correct) decisions to employ a narrow or a broad time frame when considering the guilt of a defendant. A narrow time frame will confine the interrogation and the appropriate arguments to the discrete period when the event at issue occurred: Did he pull the trigger or didn't he? A broader time frame takes in more of the act's antecedents—indeed undermines the act's identity as an act, as a bang-bang onetime thing—and opens up the way to a determinist argument: yes, he pulled the trigger, but he was forced to do so by circumstances.

The narrower the time frame, the fewer factors the jury is able to consider and the more restricted the arguments an attorney is able to make. The broader the time frame, the more the act disappears into its antecedents and the more factors an attorney can put in play as he makes his points. A narrow time frame implies that the act performed was intentional, a discrete choice made by an agent who, because he knew what he was doing, is responsible for its consequences. A broad time frame parcels out the intention, giving parts of it to an ever longer series of prior events. The more the intention is dispersed, the harder it is to locate it in any one moment and the easier it becomes to excuse the present actor, who, after all, is caught up in a history from which he cannot extricate himself in order to act "freely." (Milton's Adam tries to excuse his eating of the apple by making just this argument.)

Neither time frame, Kelman explains, is the natural, right one, and there is no objective way of deciding between them. It's just a matter of "interpretive constructs" that are already in place before the legal actor begins his task. "Most basic issues of the criminal law are issues of the applicability of an intentionalist model." The existence of other models is simply ignored or noted in passing. While criminal jurisprudence "*acknowledges* the plausibility of a determinist discourse . . . it *acts* as if the intentionalist discourse is ultimate, complete, coherent, and convincing" ("Interpretive Construction in the Substantive Criminal Law," *Stanford Law Review*, 1981).

Kelman's italics imply that the criminal law's prerational, rhetorical adoption of the intentionalist model is somehow culpable. But the assumption of an intentionalist model and the psychology that goes along with it—the psychology of agents who author their actions and are therefore responsible for them—is necessary to there being a criminal law at all. If you take away blameworthiness (which demands a narrow time frame), the entire machinery of criminal law is without an object and the procedures of assigning fault and determining appropriate penalties make no sense because there is no intentional act to fault or penalize. The distinction between blameworthy action and excusable/innocent action is just like the distinction between speech and action; it is easy to deconstruct it; nothing supports it but its own assertion—it is a fiction or, in Kelman's vocabulary, an interpretive construction, established rhetorically and in no other way—but without its assertion a whole line of legal inquiry and argument cannot get started.

What Kelman seems to see as an option—you can adopt a narrow time frame and an intentional model or you can choose not to—is in fact what is required if we are to have a category called criminal law. A determinist account of action in which no one really acts freely leaves no room for the questions and arguments that are the content of criminal jurisprudence and so, Kelman observes, "we simply rule out the determinist claim that 'crime is unavoidable.'" "Rule out" is not quite right, for it suggests a sequence in which you first posit criminal law and *then* figure out whether your model of it should be intentionalist or determinist; but the intentionalist model of human agency comes first and only when it is in place can something called criminal law emerge, and bring with it the restricted range of arguments the model makes possible and mandatory. If your first and ruling assumption is "crime is unavoidable," inquiries into blame and the assignment of penalties make no sense. If you want to be able to fix responsibility for a deed that one might have decided *not* to perform, the "intentionalist" model of behavior is the only way to go.

Nor is that model of human agency something the criminal lawyer selects; rather he has already presupposed it simply by virtue of assuming that criminal law is an entity and the practice of it an intelligible activity. Kelman says, "As best I can tell, we do these interpretive constructions utterly un-self-consciously." In fact, we don't *do* them at all. We are extensions of them the moment we enter this particular legal domain, and at the same time we become heirs to that domain's storehouse of arguments. The narrow limits of what I call bounded-space arguments are not chosen or designed by the practitioner; they come along with the territory and the practitioner has no choice but to use them and use no others.

The same holds true of other legal domains. In the branch of law concerned with negligence, the focus of interrogation is not blame as it is in the criminal law but responsibility; and the responsibility at issue is not responsibility for a designed harm but for a harm that has been produced accidentally. One party has suffered an injury that another party has inflicted, either by doing something (sending smoke from a chimney into a neighbor's bedroom) or by failing to do something (shovel the sidewalk or trim the overhanging branches of a tree). The legal task, then, is first to determine the nature and degree of the second party's responsibility and then to award damages or compel compensatory behavior.

As in the model underlying criminal law, the model under-lying negligence law assumes—but does not offer to prove—a picture of human capabilities and limits with respect to the infliction of harm. In that picture, it is possible to avoid com-mitting negligent acts by taking due care; harms are to some extent foreseeable; it is possible to establish a line of cause and effect between the harm suffered and the action of the defendant; the defendant's action or failure to act need not be the closest cause of the harm, but it must be proximate in the sense that but for its occurrence the harm would not have materialized; if there is an intervening cause or the plaintiff/sufferer has been a contributor to the negligence, the causal line may be attenuated or broken. The points I have just listed are not discrete concerns that just happen to have coalesced around negligence law; they follow from negligence law's basic form—the form of the injurer and the injuree and the obligation to right a wrong—as do the questions that will be asked ("Were you aware or should you have been aware of the potential danger to others posed by your act?") and the arguments that will be made ("All he had to do was shovel his walk") in the course of a trial.

Of course, it is always possible to say things like, "It's really not that simple; many more factors than seem to be recognized by tort law contribute to the doing and suffering of a harm; real people don't go around asking themselves if they are exercising due care or calculating the possible unhappy results of their actions; and besides, sometimes stuff just happens." But again the law is less directly sensitive to the myriad details of life lived in time than it is to its own categories and definitions (precisely the complaint of those like Felix Cohen who wish to jettison law's vocabulary and replace it with experience and common sense). The form a tort law case takes does not depend on the real-world characteristics of the persons caught in its toils; rather, once they enter tort law's domain, those persons take on the characteristics demanded by the form; they are the persons tort law requires them to be—careful or careless, foreseeing or inattentive, injurers or injurees—and the persons they actually are—fathers, mothers, sons, daughters, Democrats, Republicans, short, tall, thin, fat, brave, cowardly, nasty, nice—become irrelevant to the proceedings (unless, of course, these identifying marks can be shown to be pertinent to the determination of who suffered a wrong at whose hands).

So again what we have is a fictional world complete with fictional motives, fictional obligations, fictional calculations, fictional stick figures, all participating in fiction-informed deliberations. And, again, the fictional or constructed status of the law does not undermine its authority, but enhances it; artificial persons, artificial concepts, artificial rules, all combine to define (and create) a territory marked by clear routes from fact-situation A to conclusion B, with no extraneous considerations messing things up, because they have all been exiled at the beginning of the procedure. The attorney who negotiates those routes does so with arguments that are preauthorized by the law's form—its stipulation of what negligence legally involves—and avoids other arguments, which, while they might be effective in other contexts, are quite literally out of place in this one.

The Lure of Plain Meaning Once Again

In contract law the constitutive fiction is not, as it is in tort law, two parties who collide accidentally at an unintended moment of harm to one of them, but two parties who desire to engage in a transaction, and are at the outset free and equally situated with respect to the capacity to make a deal. A contract is defined legally as a bargain or exchange entered into voluntarily by persons who have an arm's-length relationship to each other. They may in fact be acquaintances or friends or relatives, but for the purpose of contract making and contract enforcing they are the party of the first part and the party of the second part, and the expectations of what they will do in the future are set by the fact of the agreement they sign (or verbally assent to or shake hands on), not by anything we know about their personalities, character, standing in the community, religious affiliation, sexual orientation, political identification, educational attainments, bodily strength, et cetera. (Although, as in tort law, these factors can become relevant if they can be shown to bear on the question of whether there was a contract in the first place.)

It follows, then, that when a legal question is raised about performance or breach, the arguments are restricted to issues of contract formation—was an offer tendered and accepted?—and contract performance. The courts typically do not inquire into the fairness of a contract or rewrite its terms so as to bring them into line with some notion of justice. It is assumed that "each party is competent to choose the terms upon which he is willing to be bound" (Carolyn Edwards, "Freedom of Contract and Fundamental Fairness for Individual Parties," *UMKC Law Review*, 2009). That assumption is of course a fiction. In the real world parties are not equally situated; some are rich, others poor; some are well informed and confident in their knowledge, others are ignorant and easily duped; some are independent and powerful, others dependent and weak; some have the upper hand and can hold out for terms that favor them, others are desperate and feel they must take anything offered. Surely, common sense would say, those and other relevant differences should be taken into account when thinking about issues like enforceability and breach.

And in fact there have been efforts, limitedly successful, to build into contract law a "concern for the uneducated and often illiterate individual who is the victim of gross inequality of bargaining power" (*Jones v. Star Credit Corp.*, 1969), but in the tug of war between strict adherence to freedom of contract and a strong concept of social duty undergirded by concepts like "unconscionability" (bargains that shock the conscience) and "good faith," freedom of contract has usually won on the reasoning that "one's right to negotiate a bargain, to exercise freedom of will, to choose a path, and to even make a bad deal must be admitted and respected" (*El Paso Natural Gas Co. v. Minco Oil & Gas Co.*, 1997). "*Must* be respected," because if it isn't, if the fiction of two parties equally free to choose the terms on which they will be bound is replaced by an inquiry into all the circumstances that surround the supposed "meeting of minds," the contract's words could be set aside and the cardinal legal virtues of stability and predictability would be threatened: "the bedrock principle of American contract law [is] that parties are free to contract as they see fit, and the courts are to enforce the agreements as written" (*Wilke v. Auto-Owners Ins. Co.*, 2003).

The phrase "agreements as written" introduces still another constitutive fiction, the fiction of plain meaning, meaning that declares itself and requires no supplemental interpretive materials to stabilize it. (You will recognize that we have already met this fiction, along with its utopian hopes, many times.) It is this view of language—literal, denotative, and objective—that informs what is known as the "parol evidence" rule, the rule that evidence outside the four corners of a contract cannot be brought in to determine its meaning, especially if that meaning is clear, unambiguous, and plain. Here, for example, is the state of Oregon's version of the rule: "When the terms of an agreement have been reduced to writing by the parties, it is to be considered as containing all those terms, and therefore there can be . . . no evidence of the terms of the agreement other than the contents of the writing."

One can easily see why the rule is attractive: it promises to hold parties to the bargain they have made and prevent one party from arguing, for example, that conversations engaged in prior to the completion of the writing should be considered part of the contract or that he or she had something else in mind and didn't quite manage to express it in written form. With the parol evidence rule in place, parties to a contract can feel confident that the agreement they entered into will be honored and not altered or rewritten by the interpretive tricks of some artful lawyer: "A strict parol evidence rule combined with a strong view of plain meaning gives . . . people psychic comfort as well as predictive stability. It is reassuring to believe that the words on a page provide order" (Peter Linzer, "The Comfort of Certainty: Plain Meaning and the Parol Evidence Rule," *Fordham Law Review*, 2002).

But while it may be reassuring to believe this, unfortunately it isn't true. As any number of contract theorists from Arthur Corbin to the present generation have pointed out, the parol evidence rule doesn't work. In fact, it can't be followed,

for if it kicks in only when the contract is complete and inte-
grated, there must be a determination that a particular contract can be characterized as complete, and in order to make
that determination you will have to bring in just the kind of
extrinsic evidence that is supposedly barred. If the nonam-
biguity of the contract is established through argument and
interpretation, the evidence that now cannot be introduced
according to the rule has already been introduced in the effort
to figure out just how the rule should be applied.

Here is the Supreme Court of Arizona making just that
point: "the court must first decide what the agreement says
and, as a preliminary matter, must decide if it could reasonably
be interpreted in different ways, given the language, and the
factual context surrounding the making of the agreement. . . .
After all, the purpose is to produce the contract result the parties intended" (*Taylor v. State Farm Mutual Auto Insurance Co.*,
1993). While the language of the contract is certainly a factor
in specifying what it means, if the point is as the court says it
is—to honor the intentions of the parties—evidence of that
intention should not be barred just because some impossible-
to-follow formalistic rule says so: "In determining the intent
of the parties the court looks to the written contract as well as
to extrinsic evidence regarding the parties' intent at the time
the contract was made" (*Municipality of Anchorage v. Gentile*,
1966). The Alaska Supreme Court speaks here in the accents
of Corbin, who delivered this emphatic rejection of the parol
evidence rule and plain meaning in his *Corbin on Contracts*
(1950): "it can hardly be insisted on too often that language
at its best is always a defective and uncertain instrument, that

words do not define themselves, that terms and sentences in a contract, a deed, or a will do not apply themselves." As Peter Linzer puts it, "The agreement between the parties is the contract, and to limit it to the written words and to treat the parties' actual intent as irrelevant is to invest the writing with a potency similar to what primitive faith does" ("The Comfort of Certainty").

The faith may be primitive, but it is still clung to despite everything Linzer, Corbin, and a host of legal commentators say. In the course of detailing for twenty-five pages the almost universal derision directed by contract theorists at the concept of plain meaning, Margaret Kniffen (who writes in the course of revising Corbin's chapter on interpretation) acknowledges that "the 'plain meaning' rule is adhered to by a majority of the jurisdictions in the United States."

Of course it is! As we have seen, the fact that a useful and necessary fiction has been exposed as one is no reason to abandon it. Even if the plain meaning rule cannot be followed—because there is no such thing as plain meaning in the required sense of a meaning that words deliver in and of themselves independently of context or intention—the plain meaning rule performs a real service: first, it sends a message to drafters—choose your words carefully; second, it stands as a caution to interpreters who know they are being held to a standard even if the standard can't be met; and third, it acts as what has been called a "regulative ideal," an ideal that stands as a beacon and a constraint even if it has not yet been realized and may never be realized. The repeated invocation of the plain meaning rule says to legal practitioners and to the world at large, "We are serious about what we do and we take care to do it in a way that, we hope, instills confidence in our procedures and our integrity." The incoherence of the plain meaning rule is less important than the force it has simply by being part of the lawyer's rhetorical arsenal; its very existence is itself an argument, even though arguments based on its invocation always, and necessarily, fail.

Even Corbin, after declaring roundly that there are no objective meanings and no fixed and settled rules, says, "Nevertheless the 'law' consists of 'rules,'" and "they are not to be scorned" for "without them the world would be a chaotic and guideless world, with every man acting in accordance with his own vagrant emotion and desire" ("Sixty-Eight Years at Law," *University of Kansas Law Review*, 1964). Or, in other words, plain meanings and fixed rules such as the parol evidence rule are fictions, but they are fictions that allow us to set up a system of self-regulation and guidance in the absence of which we would all be at sea and at one another's throats. And this remains true even if the regulations are porous and the guidance they offer is always vulnerable to challenge and revision. Just as there would be no First Amendment law without the speech/action distinction, no negligence law without the presumption that it is possible to fix responsibility narrowly, and no criminal law without the fiction of acts performed discretely by a freely choosing malefactor, so would there be no contract law if the knowledge that words are malleable and intentions infinitely interpretable were put at the forefront of every stage in contract negotiation and adjudication. Philosophy is one thing and its truths are often powerful; but they cannot be allowed to structure and constrain a practice that can survive only if philosophical truths are temporarily forgotten or at least bracketed while the practice goes its self-authorizing, nonphilosophical way.

What the Law's Arguments Leave Out

The law's way, if determinedly pursued, can exact a price on those who are caught up in its fictions. In a poignant essay, Anthony Alfieri reports on the anguished experience of a client, a foster mother, who, in her own words, recalls, "They shut off my lights in November, when my kids' food stamps were first reduced. . . . I had taken the money from my public assistance check to buy food for that month for me and my kids" ("Reconstructive Poverty Law Practice: Learning Lessons of Client Narrative," *Yale Law Journal*, 1991).

Her story, as she tells it, is one of hardship, fortitude, and resourcefulness, and, above all, love. But when it gets translated into the story her lawyer tells in court, the emphasis changes and the story becomes one of dependency. This happens because the poverty lawyer listens with "legal ears" and fits what he hears into the prefabricated categories that are both the tools and the limitations of his profession. These categories, says Alfieri, "objectify the client in a dependent role," the role of someone who is either a victim or incompetent or enfeebled. Left out entirely are those aspects of the client's story that are "empowering"—the stirring narrative of "the struggle to accommodate and overthrow subjugation." That narrative does not survive the lawyer's transubstantiation of it into something he can put before a court: "When distorted by the lawyer's interpretive practices . . . the client's narratives appear irrelevant to the lawyer's task of storytelling." Alfieri's verdict on this process is firm and starkly negative: "Lawyer storytelling falsifies client story when lawyer narratives silence and displace client narratives."

This may be too harsh because it suggests a malevolent design presided over either by the individual lawyer or the profession personified. (It is sometimes said that law is a conspiracy against the laity.) In fact, what is happening is less sinister, though no less disheartening and disappointing if you are the client who wants to hear her story told as she lived it. Like any other discipline or enterprise, the law views the world through the lens of its central purpose—the purpose, broadly speaking, of doing justice by righting wrongs and protecting rights. Therefore, when fact situations come into the law's ken, it will configure them into narratives that have the emphases, distinctions, oppositions, problems, and remedies its own purpose-informed vocabulary names, and by naming, legitimates as legal. In order to successfully operate within the precincts of the law, the lawyer must present in its forums narratives that the relevant authorities will recognize as belonging "here"—in the courtroom, in the negotiating room, in the grand jury room—and not "there"—in the boardroom or the bedroom or the barroom or the street.

"Thinking like a lawyer" is a cliché that has become an accusation: lawyers live in their own world and are cut off from the lived world of their clients. But what you want when you hire a lawyer is someone so completely at home in the world of the discipline that he or she can immediately, and with only a little bit of reflection, discern which weapons in the professional arsenal—an arsenal composed largely of arguments—can be deployed in your service. The lawyer you hope will win the argument for you must be the lawyer who knows what the arguments are, who knows which arguments will fly and which will not, who knows what parts of your tale can be translated into legal points and what parts of your tale, however dear and important they may be to you, must be discarded. In the bounded space of legal argument, not everything can be heard or said, even if in the grander scheme of things—grander, that is, than any professional game—what is left out is regarded by some as life itself.

CHAPTER 5

ACADEMIC ARGUMENTS

◆─────◆

I Said That First: Being Original

IF YOU WANT to make an argument in the academy, either as a professor or a student, you will be no less constrained than you are in court. The difference is that in the bounded space of legal argument the constraints are written down, while in the bounded space of academic argument they typically are not.

We can open a window onto the world of academic argument by considering the idea of plagiarism, usually defined as signing your name to, and thereby claiming as your own, the words, images, or ideas of another. In 1976 an essay of mine ("Interpreting the Variorum," *Critical Inquiry*) was published in which I coined the term "interpretive community."

An interpretive community is not made up of persons who, because they share some of the same ideas and aims, get together and form a club, as *Star Trek* fans do. Rather, an interpretive community is made up of those who, by virtue of training, experience, and practice, have internalized the norms of some purposive enterprise—law, education, politics, plumbing—to the point where they see with its eyes and walk in its ways without having to think about it. Interpretive community members are not independent agents who self-consciously choose to think and act in a certain way; if they are deeply embedded in the community they have no choice; the world just appears to them already organized by the emphases and urgencies that are the community's content.

When, for example, my students and I enter the classroom, we don't have to ask ourselves about the significance of the arrangement of the room, about the seats facing forward in the direction of a podium, about the behaviors we can and cannot indulge in while the class is meeting, or about a thousand other things. Situated as we are in the interpretive community called "higher education in America"—a community located not in a particular physical space but in a set of practices—knowledge of what everything in the scene of instruction means and is for just comes with the territory (we don't have to reach for it) or, rather, comes with having become a native of the territory. It is the kind of knowledge often referred to as "know-how" or "horse sense."

In a short time the interpretive community idea caught on and was applied to different problems in different disciplines. After a while many people forgot where the term originated and used it without attributing it to me. In effect, I was being plagiarized all the time, and it isn't getting any better as more and more scholars drop the words "interpretive community" into their essays and books without any acknowledgment. (Wikipedia, at least, gives me proper credit.)

Why am I distressed at the casual appropriation by many of a two-word phrase? After all, isn't it an honor to have one's ideas become so much a feature of the disciplinary landscape that they belong to everyone? The answer has to do with the system of currency in the academy. In that system big ideas count for more than small points made in the course of an argument, and as it has turned out, "interpretive community" is a big idea (with an obvious resemblance to Thomas Kuhn's "paradigm," Pierre Bourdieu's "habitus," and Michael Polanyi's category of "tacit knowledge"). If you are known as the originator, and therefore the proprietor, of a big idea, your academic stock is to some extent secure; for that identification goes along with you even if you have not touched or developed the idea in years, much as the winner of an Academy Award is introduced as one long after he or she has made any well-received films, and much as an ex-senator is still addressed as Senator even though it's been decades since he or she was in office. So if there is a conference on the big idea or a journal issue devoted to it, you will likely be invited to contribute, and even if you are not, you can still count on your name being mentioned (not always in praise, but that doesn't matter) many times.

All of this (and much else) follows from the fact that what is valued in the academy is originality. Both plagiarism as a culpable act and the academic enterprise as a field of competition make sense only if originality is presupposed as a possibility and a value. At first glance, originality seems to be a perfectly ordinary notion understood by everyone: you are original if you do or say or come up with something no one else has said or done or thought of. That something, whatever it is—a computer chip, a new art form, an innovative surgical technique, an analytical model, a better argument, a better mousetrap—is yours. You own it, have rights to it, and in the world of patent and copyright you are to some extent able to control its use and reproduction. So when I came up with the idea of an interpretive community (as a way of outflanking both those who believe that meaning resides in the text and those who believe that meaning resides in the reader), I was suddenly the possessor of something of value, something others might borrow and modify to the extent that they found it helpful in their professional labors. I couldn't patent the idea or copyright it, but I could regard it as a piece of "intellectual property" and require as a matter of professional courtesy, if not as a matter of law, that users acknowledge my ownership when invoking the phrase. (As I have noted, that hasn't quite worked out.)

So that's the basic economy of the academy: you advance and prosper to the extent that the solutions you offer to intellectual puzzles are found persuasive and are subsequently credited to you as their originator. Promotions, honors, and influence follow.

For some time, however, the components that make up this "originality picture" have been under challenge. First of all, the idea of a single author whose willed intention produces a text or an image that can be identified as "his" or "hers" has been attacked by philosophers, art historians, historians of science, theorists of the Internet, literary critics, and a host of others often influenced by essays such as Roland Barthes's "The Death of the Author" and Michel Foucault's "What Is an Author?" The basic idea in these essays is that language, rather than being an instrument available for use by individuals who choose what to say and mean, is a "ready-made dictionary" (the phrase is Barthes's), a system of differences or binaries that precedes, enables, and constrains the production of intelligible speech acts. The individual who would speak must go through that system in order to form assertions; he can't step "outside" the system in a gesture of freedom; he must attach himself to its prefabricated meanings, meanings that speak through him as opposed to doing his bidding. Rather than being the master of language, he ventriloquizes it; rather than engaging in the act of *self*-expression, he is the vehicle of language's expression of itself. In Barthes's words, "it is language that speaks, not the author," who is merely its local and temporary habitation.

It follows that originality is not a claim one can make, given that one can say only what the system allows one to say; one can say only what has been said already. When John Milton begins his pastoral elegy "Lycidas" with the words "Yet once more," he acknowledges his status as a mere relay or node traversed by texts and meanings he cannot sign his name to as an "only begetter." "Yet once more" means "Here I am again (even if it is the first time for me) singing the themes and notes given to me by the tradition that takes me over, the tradition I now voice not as a willed choice but as a necessity that befalls every singer who would strum the pastoral lyre." Mikhail Bakhtin drives the point home: "language is not a neutral medium that passes freely and easily into the private property of the speaker's intentions; it is populated, overpopulated, with the intentions of others" (*Speech Genres and Other Late Essays*, 1986). You can't be a freestanding self in charge of intentions that belong exclusively to you.

If the independent, meaning-originating self is a myth, so necessarily is the unique textual object that supposedly stands as the fixed and visible guarantor of the meaning the self has supposedly originated. Texts are not bounded, self-enclosed entities waiting to be claimed. All texts are collages of previous texts—you can't start from scratch—and no text has the fixity and stability—sameness of shape and significance through time—that would be required for it to be an ownable entity. A text cannot emerge into visibility against its own background; it becomes salient, capable of being distinguished as an entity, only when it is seen in relation to the innumerable texts that came before it or sit alongside it. A single page of an annotated edition of "Lycidas" might display two lines of text surrounded by thirty-three lines of sources and analogues. A text's identity is relational, not frontal; it is what it is (or isn't) because it is like and unlike other texts, which are in turn like and unlike other texts, and on and on; it has no self-identity. As Jean Baudrillard puts it, "A truly unique, absolute object such that it has no antecedents and is no way dispersed in some series or other—such an object is unthinkable" (*The System of Objects*, 2005).

Baudrillard's statement finds a contemporary reflection and confirmation in the notion of "hypertext." A hypertext is not a freestanding bounded object that the reader enters at one end and exits at the other. Rather, it is "always open, borderless, unfinished and unfinishable, capable of infinite extension" (George Landow, *Hypertext 2.0*, 1997). One reads not in a straight line, but back and forth, up and down, taking detour after detour by way of serial clicking until detours are the main path. Old questions like "What's the point being made?" or "What is the unifying principle here" or "What, exactly, is the author saying?" are no longer pertinent. The point, if there is one, is constantly shifting; unity cannot be claimed for a shape always being transformed; there is no author, no centering intelligence that can either be blamed or take the credit for what issues. The text (if that word can still be used intelligibly) is written by no one and by everyone: "Hypertext lends itself to texts that are an assemblage of text blocks and images borrowed from other sites and brought together through pastiche" (Barbara Warnick, "Hypertext," *Encyclopedia of Rhetoric*, 2001).

Pastiche, mosaic, collage, miscellany, kaleidoscope—these familiar terms acquire a new intensity and centrality in the Internet world, where fluidity and multivocality are not the exceptions to the assumed standard of single-authored writings, but the rule. In that world all texts are interconnected and no text has its own shape, the independent agency of authors is an illusion, the vocabulary of originality and ownership is a mistake, the charge of plagiarism makes no sense, and students understandably feel justified in appropriating without acknowledgment whatever they find useful because, after all, everything is "common knowledge," knowledge belonging to no one and therefore belonging to everyone. Here is Franco Berardi's description of this high-tech utopian (or dystopian, depending on where you stand) vision: "no object, no existent, and no person: only aggregates, temporary compositional figures" that are "mutational, transient, frayed and indefinable" (*The Soul at Work*, 2009).

Originality Rises from Its Own Ashes

And yet—and this is the point I have been winding toward—those like Berardi, who are elaborating and celebrating this brave new world where the claim of originality can never be cashed in, sign the essays they write, gather together in manifestos and anthologies advertised as offering a new saving truth, and in general comport themselves as academic entrepreneurs who have something to sell and therefore something they own. I don't intend this as a criticism. The fact that these authors-despite-themselves are claiming originality for their arguments against originality is not so much a contradiction as it is an inevitable consequence of having entered the arena of academic argument, where the imperative is to be the originator of something new and where the assumption is that you wouldn't be putting yourself forward were you not making that claim.

The headnote of a blog entry (*Jerz's Literacy Weblog*, jerz
.setonhill.edu/writing/academic1) makes my point concisely:
"Academic Argument: Evidence-based Defense of a Non-
obvious Position." "Non-obvious" is the key. It means "most
people mistakenly think X or haven't even thought of Y, but
I know better and I have the goods, and that's why you should
listen to me." That is what you have to do to earn your bona
fides as an academic: enter an ongoing conversation about a
topic deemed to be important—not important in the larger
world (although it may be), but important in the academic
world—survey the arguments now competing for attention,
and put forward an argument of your own that corrects the
others or outflanks them (by bringing them together in a
"higher synthesis"), or reconfigures the field by arguing that
your predecessors have asked the wrong questions; you, of
course, have the right ones.

You might think this is just common knowledge, but it
isn't. It is knowledge peculiar to the province we call academic life; and it is knowledge students who enter that province as novices will have to learn, often with difficulty. They
can turn for help to Gerald Graff and Cathy Birkenstein's *They
Say, I Say: The Moves That Matter in Academic Writing* (2006).
Graff and Birkenstein begin with a simple premise: "academic
writing is argumentative writing, and we believe that to argue
well you need to do more than assert your own ideas. You need
to enter a conversation, using what others say (or might say) as
a launching pad or sounding board for your own ideas." The
conversation you enter has been going on for a long time and
it will be marked by the formulation of key problems, a small

number of competing resolutions, an equally small number of influential voices, arguments that are in the ascendancy, arguments that have been discarded, arguments that are considered taboo, authoritative texts, long-standing puzzles, and a great deal more, awareness of which must be built into your performance. Thus the "They say, I say" formula, a formula I followed at the beginning of this paragraph when I said, "You might think this is just common knowledge, but . . ."

Graff and Birkenstein write for undergraduates, but they are not the only ones who need help. Years ago a graduate student from another college came to ask my advice about a dissertation she was planning to write. Her topic, the relationship between Supreme Court decisions and the history of race relations, was a reasonable one and her enthusiasm for it was evident. I asked her to write an outline or prospectus stating her thesis and the arguments she would make to support it. When I looked at what she had given me I found that her writing (and thinking) was driven by moral outrage rather than scholarly inquiry. Instead of allowing her conclusion to follow from the evidence, she began with her conclusion (that the Court was complicit with everything bad that had ever happened) and then proceeded to reaffirm it in every paragraph.

I told her that if this was to be a piece of *academic* writing, she would have to first make a case for why anyone in the field, as opposed to someone she was talking to in a coffee shop, would be interested in what she had to say. That case would have to include a survey of previous scholarship (always treated with respect even in the act of disagreeing with it), especially the scholarship of established leaders, and an account of how what she proposed to do would fit in, where "fitting in" was understood to include revising and even disrupting received wisdom.

Once that was done, I told her, she could put forward analyses of the cases she believed were significant, analyses that might in time lead to the conclusion she had already come to. I pointed out that in the course of working through the material she might be moved to revise that conclusion; scholarly work is in part defined by the possibility that gathering and arranging the evidence might bring you to a place different from the one you had hoped to reach. An indictment of the court might be the earned result of the materials she marshaled; it shouldn't be the starting point to which the materials were made to conform. I added that if she brought in vocabularies and models from other disciplines to develop and buttress her case, she would have to make clear that she was genuinely conversant with these disciplines and not just borrowing phrases in an exercise of window dressing. In short, I gave her the short course in academic argument.

It didn't take. The revision she brought back to me was cosmetically improved, but right beneath the surface were the same moral urgency, premature judgment, and already-cooked conclusion that had bothered me in the first place. I explained it all over again and sent her away to make another try. This time, she didn't come back and I don't blame her. She wasn't unintelligent—far from it! She just didn't want to do academic work, strictly speaking; she wanted to do social justice and she happened to be in a program where political advocacy and academic work were not distinct categories. What I was telling her just didn't jibe with what she was hearing from her teachers and fellow students.

Now the very fact of such a program presents a difficulty for my assertion that academic work has a distinctive shape in relationship to which some kinds of argument are obligatory and other kinds suspect. If entire departments regard as legitimate the kinds of argument I say are not properly academic, my category of "properly academic" is in danger of becoming idiosyncratic and tendentious. I am led by this example, and by others that could be instanced, to a refinement of my description of bounded-argument spaces.

First, not all bounded spaces are the same; in some the boundaries are not as rigorously policed as they are in others. In the law, as we saw, the kinds of arguments that can and cannot be offered are established by codified rules, and the rules are enforced by judges who can say "inadmissible" and make it stick. In the academy—including the legal academy (it is important to keep in mind the distinction between the practice of law and the study of the practice of law)—the rules are often understood decorums rather than regulations backed by an authority capable of enforcing them. If a lawyer wants to introduce evidence of bad prior acts, a judge will not allow it except in carefully delineated circumstances. If a college or university or law school teacher wants to turn a classroom into a staging ground for his or her political views, there may not be anything to stop him or her unless some students complain to the administration, the administration takes the complaint seriously, and a committee impaneled to hear such complaints issues a firm judgment. (The likelihood of this sequence occurring is small.) So it is possible in the academy as it is not in the law for there to be a unit or program that is in good standing even though it flouts the generally understood norms of the enterprise.

To be sure, there are gatekeeping mechanisms in the academic world that operate to send away work that rather than seeking to advance our understanding of an issue seeks to advance a political agenda and turn students and readers into activists. Learned journals often serve that function, as do those who organize panels at regional and national meetings. But if the learned journals are keeping you and your friends out and labeling what you do "unprofessional" or "nonacademic," you can start a journal of your own and devote its first issue to explaining why the current definitions of "professional" and "academic" are too narrow and mask an ideological position that is not announcing itself. In the academy it is always possible to set up a "rogue" territory where what is done is frowned upon by the conservative establishment. The graduate student who asked me for help came from such a territory.

How the Academy Survives All Assaults, Even Those It Sponsors

What this means is that what is and is not a proper academic argument is itself something continually being argued about. The argument can even extend to the point of calling the entire enterprise into question. Professional norms in the

legal academy preside over arguments about their own effi-
cacy; reasons are given for doubting the very existence of
legal reasoning. In the early part of the twentieth century,
self-described "legal realists" inveighed against legal rules,
legal concepts, and legal autonomy, characterizing the whole
supposedly rational structure as a sham, a myth, a deliberate
obfuscation, and urging lawyers and judges to attend to the
facts on the ground and the needs and lives of real persons,
all of which, they said, are bypassed when abstract categories
speak not to any realities but to each other in a spectacularly
empty manner. Later in the century, members of the Critical Legal Studies movement added to the realist arguments
the postmodern, deconstructionist arguments that language is
irremediably indeterminate; that rules, no matter how finely
drawn, do not yield stable and predictable outcomes; that
because the deployment of legal terms can lead to any outcome the manipulator of those terms desires there is no such
things as the rule of law; that the distinction between law and
power cannot be maintained; that everything standard legal
doctrine wants to keep out—politics, subjectivity, ideology—
is already in; and that the whole bankrupt, shaky edifice is
designed to further the interests of the haves and keep the
have-nots in their place. (Mark Kelman declared that law professors are only "a kiss away from panic when they don't have
a bunch of overawed students to kick around" ["Trashing,"
Stanford Law Review, 1984].)

And yet, the force of these arguments aimed at blowing up
the establishment was more than a little blunted by the fact
that they were appearing in the very establishment pages of

law reviews at Stanford, Harvard, Wisconsin, Texas, and Yale. Although a lot of noise was made by both the purveyors of these radical pronouncements and those who darkly warned about the "death of the law," when all the dust settled, the day to day work of the enterprise was being done in the same way and the same subjects, divided into traditional categories, were being taught in a manner that would have been familiar in outline to Christopher Columbus Langdell, the originator of the "case method" in the late nineteenth century.

In the liberal arts world, the assaults on the assumptions, methodologies, and very structure of the enterprise were even fiercer. From the late '60s on, we were told there is no such thing as a text; we were told that there is no such thing as the fact of the matter; indeed there is no such thing as a fact; we were told that history is a text and because it is a text and not a "thing" it cannot be recovered; it can only be *re*-covered; we were told that philosophy fails because it has no vantage point—no "subject position"—from which to pronounce; we were told that anthropology cannot be responsibly practiced because its very touch corrupts its object; we were told that political science is a misnomer for there is nothing scientific about it; we were told that the boundaries between the academy and the "real world" are not only permeable; they are socially constructed by parties with an investment in maintaining the status quo. Everywhere it went, the corrosive touch of postmodern theory seemed to lay waste to the disciplinary landscape.

And yet, when things quieted down and the voices preaching apocalypse and the counter-voices sounding the alarm subsided, all the disciplines and departments were still standing, doing recognizable business under the old rubrics, although the business was somewhat changed by the very arguments the establishment had pushed away. As Andrew Abbott has observed, "The departmental structure of the American university has remained largely unchanged since its creation between 1890 and 1910" (*Chaos of Disciplines*, 2001). An academic discipline can tolerate any challenge so long as the challenge is conducted within its precincts. Supposedly subversive arguments are absorbed into the very intellectual structures they claim to overthrow. Challenges to the very core of the enterprise tend to operate on the margins, where they are regarded almost as entertainments ("Did you hear what those postmodern nuts are saying now?"), as Old Man Discipline just keeps rolling along.

Of course renewal is always part of the discipline's project, and in the name of renewal disruptive ideas are given a hearing. But when renewal threatens to turn into revolution and the overturning of everything in sight, the ranks close because practitioners who signed on to a particular project want to continue doing what they were trained to do even in the face of arguments they themselves have made against the possibility of doing it.

Thus while disciplines exhibit a succession of different faces over time, something familiar survives every new wave. Each discipline, Stephen Toulmin explains, "though mutable, normally displays a recognizable continuity" despite the many things that have changed (*Human Understanding, Volume 1,*

1972). And that is why even when the account of the academy as an ivory tower where contemplation, not action, is the goal has been roundly denounced by a generation of scholars, it remains firmly in place. This, say Tony Becher and Paul R. Trowler, is "one of the most curious" of the paradoxes that abound in academia—"the apparent coexistence of radical chic with entrenched conservatism" (*Academic Tribes and Territories*, 2001). It's not curious or a paradox at all; it follows perfectly from an enterprise whose basic structure of inquiry is clung to even when that inquiry turns up results that seem to threaten its foundation.

Holocaust Deniers Need Not Apply

It is within that entrenched conservatism (and with due allowance for dissenters trying to push the envelope) that one can confidently pronounce on what arguments are acceptable and unacceptable in the academy: Generally, an academic argument must be academic; it shouldn't be political or therapeutic or exhortatory. It can, however, have political, therapeutic, and exhortatory effects, as long as those effects are not aimed at by the instructor. Something a student studies might well lead him or her to a career choice or to a political commitment or to a personal revelation, but those outcomes are contingent—they may or may not occur—and, because contingent, cannot be the motivating hope of disciplinary instruction. The appropriate motivating hope is a more modest one—that at the end of the semester the student will have mastered a body of materials and become familiar with the debates surrounding those materials, as well as with the analytic techniques and models employed by up-to-date researchers in the field.

That's actually a lot to accomplish in fourteen or fifteen weeks, and, properly pursued, the task leaves no room for engaging in arguments about whether we should withdraw from the Middle East or legalize prostitution or adopt a single-payer medical care system. Those and related arguments can be *studied*, that is, analyzed, compared, traced to their sources, historically situated, et cetera, but they ought not to be *fought out* in the classroom with a view to reaching a conclusion that would lead to action in the world. Fighting arguments out in an action-oriented way is what is done at the United Nations, in legislatures, and in meetings at the State Department and the Department of Defense; it is not what is, or should be, done in classrooms where (pace Karl Marx) the mandate is not to change the world, but to understand it. Political topics are fine (indeed any topic is fine), but they should not be taught politically.

Although theoretically any topic is ripe for academic consideration and debate, some arguments do not make it into the arena. The academy has a list of subjects that are not considered to be candidates for serious attention, although they can be candidates for membership in the equivalent of the academic "freak show." First on the list is Holocaust denial, which in the academy occupies the same category as round-earth denial and astrology, although in the nonacademic world it attracts passionate adherents. In every country, there are those who believe passionately that the Holocaust is a myth perpetrated by Zionist Jews for political and monetary reasons, and they proclaim their belief, accompanied by reams of evidence, in journals, on websites, at conferences, and in videos. The roster of Holocaust deniers contains historians, heads of state, public intellectuals, and entertainment stars. Of course there are historians, heads of state, public intellectuals, and entertainment stars on the other side, and one might expect that the debate would be just the ticket for a university classroom where, it is often said, the search for truth is to be conducted in a spirit of open inquiry with no holds barred. Here is Canadian lawyer Barbara Kulaszka making just that point on the website of the Institute for Historical Review, a Holocaust denial organ: "Let this issue be settled as all great historical controversies are resolved: through free inquiry and open debate in our journals, newspapers, and classrooms" (2014).

Not this controversy, however. Holocaust denial has been rejected as a respectable position in nearly all Western democracies, many of which have declared it *malum in se*—evil in and of itself—and passed laws prohibiting and criminalizing the dissemination of its arguments. If the United States were such a country, the absence of Holocaust deniers in the academy would be easily explained: it would be illegal to make their arguments (as opposed, again, to studying them), and universities are not in the habit of hiring lawbreakers. But denying the Holocaust is perfectly legal in the United States, where the First Amendment has been consistently interpreted by the courts as forbidding "viewpoint discrimination"; therefore Holocaust deniers, like astrologists, must be allowed to have their say.

How is it then that you won't find any Holocaust deniers having their say in history departments? (You might find persons who deny the Holocaust teaching in departments, like electrical engineering, where neither denial nor affirmation is pertinent to the subject matter; the academy doesn't want to keep out people who *believe* disreputable things; it wants to keep out people who *teach* disreputable things.) The answer is that the discipline has decided that rather than being a legitimate form of historical "revisionism," as deniers claim, Holocaust denial is just the dressing up of lies and distortions in academic garb. In 1991, the American Historical Association said as much when it issued this statement: "No serious historian questions that the Holocaust took place."

Now you might read that as saying "as historians we've looked into the matter, gathered evidence, conducted polls, sent out questionnaires, et cetera, and what we've found is that no academic holding a position in a history department questions that the Holocaust took place." But in fact the statement follows not from empirical research but from a stipulative definition of what the phrase "serious historian" means: it means someone who affirms the Holocaust. If you deny it, you will not receive an appointment to a history department no matter what your credentials, and it is no surprise that when the AHA comes looking for deniers, it doesn't find any. The association cites as independent evidence a condition it has decreed: "No serious historian questions that the Holocaust took place." It's the academy declaring, with no other justification than the institutional force it exerts, that we're not going to give this stuff the time of day. You can profess Holocaust denial arguments in the coffee shop, in the board-room, in the bedroom, in the street, but you can't profess them as a professor and still be one. (You can of course study Holocaust denial as a regrettable cultural phenomenon, but that's quite another thing.)

What this shows is that despite the familiar claim that the academy is dedicated to open inquiry, it is not, in fact, com-mitted to giving every idea a hearing, no more than a court is committed to considering every argument offered to it. The academy is dedicated to inquiry into the topics it deems prop-erly academic—yes, the process is circular—and it will send ideas it has judged to be off the wall away without so much as a hearing.

The fate suffered by Holocaust deniers has also befallen those who believe that the plays attributed to Shakespeare were actually written by Edward De Vere, 17th Earl of Ox-ford (or Christopher Marlowe or Francis Bacon or Queen Elizabeth I). Here there is a tradition of inquiry and argu-ment going back hundreds of years and attracting all man-ner of adherents, including Mark Twain, Walt Whitman, and Henry James. Serious discussions of the topic have occurred in the pages of respectable middle-brow journals and on TV shows, and 2011 saw a major film (featuring A-list actors such as Vanessa Redgrave and Derek Jacobi, himself a parti-san of the De Vere cause) dramatizing the case for De Vere's authorship. Nevertheless, the academic Shakespeare industry remains unimpressed, even contemptuous, and while it may not be entirely accurate to say that "no serious literary student of the period questions that Shakespeare wrote his plays," it is accurate enough: as things stand now, you're not going to win your academic spurs riding that horse.

Creationists Need Not Apply

A third example of an argument that will not be taken seriously in the academy although it is made by many in the larger society is creationism, also known as intelligent design or creation science. This last designation pinpoints the issue: is creationism a legitimate scientific thesis or is it a piece of religious dogma pretending to be science? The assumption behind the question—an assumption held by many though not by all—is that creationism and science, or at least that part of science known as the theory of evolution, are antithetical. In the early years of the controversy, creationism was understood both by its proponents and its detractors to be firmly grounded in religious belief and in the fear that Darwinism, with its vocabulary of "random mutation" and "natural selection," was a threat to the sovereignty, if not the very existence, of God. (If natural selection does it all, who needs a God to explain anything?) Religious believers looked at the world and found in the precision and regularities of its structures not randomness but evidence of design; and if there is design, they reasoned, there must be a designer, and the only real candidate for that role is the God who created the universe in a sequence of acts set down in the book of Genesis.

For these believers, to attack Darwinism was to affirm God over "godless science," and it was in those terms that the issue was framed in the popular imagination and on such occasions as the famous "monkey" trial, *Scopes v. State* (1927).

Although the creationist position fared well in public opinion polls, the efforts of its proponents to embed it in public instruction by passing laws requiring that it be taught in science classes (either exclusively or in tandem with evolution) ran up against the First Amendment prohibition of any law tending to establish a religion. If the appropriate goal of the public schools is to provide "a more comprehensive science curriculum," that goal, the Supreme Court declared, "is not furthered either by outlawing the teaching of evolution or by requiring the teaching of creation science" (*Edwards v. Aguillard*, 1987). What would be furthered would be the interests of religion, and that the state cannot constitutionally do.

The response of the creationist community had already been developed before *Edwards v. Aguillard* was decided. Rather than declaring that biblical truth should trump the truths proclaimed by science, anti-Darwinists began to assert that creationism *is* science and can be supported by scientific evidence. This line of argument was fashioned by engineer Henry M. Morris and his associates at the Institute for Creation Research and extended by then law student Wendell Bird, who declared in a *Yale Law Journal* essay that a defense of creationism "could be constructed from scientific discussion of empirical evidence divorced from theological reasoning" ("Freedom of Religion and Science Instruction in

Public Schools," 1978). In the following years, the defense was mounted in great detail and refuted in even greater detail. Finally, the issue was fully joined in a landmark 2005 case, *Kitzmiller v. Dover Area School District*. In that case Judge John E. Jones delivered an opinion that roundly rejected the arguments of creationists, now flying the banner of intelligent design (ID), to be doing science: "We find that ID is not science and cannot be adjudged a valid acceptable scientific theory as it has failed to publish in peer-reviewed journals, engage in research or testing and gain acceptance in the scientific community."

Now Judge Jones is not a scientist, so where does his conviction that ID is not science come from? It comes, he tells us, from the judgment of the peer-reviewed journals. But who are the peers? They are mainstream scholars already committed to the exclusion of ID from their playground. And what does failing "to gain acceptance in the scientific community" mean? It means, Judge Jones explains, that "not a single expert witness over the course of the six-week trial identified one major scientific association, society, or organization that endorsed ID as science." Chief among those he cites is the American Association for the Advancement of Science, the "largest organization of scientists in this country." Can you imagine that? The organization dedicated to the advancement of establishment science has not endorsed the militantly anti-establishment program of ID. What a surprise! The deck is stacked just as it was by the American Historical Association when it pointed to the fact that no serious historian questions the Holocaust as if it proved something, whereas all it proved was that the American Historical Association is very powerful.

Witnesses for the losing side in *Kitzmiller* included at least one credentialed, but controversial, scientist (Michael Behe) and one prominent sociologist of knowledge (Steven Fuller), but what they said wasn't going to be seriously considered by a judge who declared that "since the scientific revolution of the sixteenth and seventeenth centuries, science has been limited to the search for natural causes." That's just the trouble, Fuller explained in his testimony. The presence of a dominant paradigm means that science tends "to be governed by a kind of, to put it bluntly, ruling elite" who want to keep things as they are (Trial Transcript, day 15). "Science," he added, "has to close ranks, has to be dogmatic and . . . has to start excluding people" who don't display the proper beliefs, a strategy of exclusion that seems not very different from the exclusions mandated by religion.

The philosopher Thomas Nagel makes just that point when he observes that the assumption by anti-creationists that ID couldn't possibly be true seems less a conclusion reached by scientific method than an article of faith. It might be said, he continues, "that both the mention of ID in a biology class and its exclusion would seem to depend on religious assumptions" ("Public Education and Intelligent Design," *Philosophy & Public Affairs*, 2008). Justice Antonin Scalia had flirted with the same conclusion in his *Edwards v. Aguillard* dissent when he cited "ample uncontradicted evidence that 'creation science' is a body of scientific knowledge rather than revealed belief." Scalia reports (without either endorsing or rejecting) the argument made by the supporters of Louisiana's Balanced Treatment for Creation-Science and Evolution-Science in Public School Instruction Act: "The body of scientific evidence supporting creation science is as strong as that supporting evolution" and may "be stronger." It's just that teachers "have been brainwashed by an entrenched scientific establishment to whom evolution is like a 'religion.'"

Scalia's friendly rehearsal of pro–creation science views did not sway Judge Jones (who certainly knew his fellow conservative jurist's dissent) because as a non-scientist the Supreme Court justice had the wrong credentials. It is a feature of bounded argument spaces that in addition to restrictions on the arguments one can make, there are restrictions on who can make them and receive a respectful hearing. An uncredentialed reader of *Paradise Lost*—a reader without a Ph.D. in English Renaissance literature—might come up with an interpretation of Milton's epic more innovative and interesting than mine, but mine is the one that will be noticed and discussed in the learned journals because I am a member (and past president) of the Milton Society of America. In bounded-argument spaces, expertise always trumps, and that is why Judge Jones ratifies what the experts have told him even though he is hearing something else from an eminent sociologist and a Supreme Court justice, not to mention millions of religious citizens, many bishops and cardinals, and a pope. He is saying, "I'll go with the American Association for the Advancement of Science," and this is perfectly reasonable in a culture where authority is professionally—that is, rhetorically—established.

Given all this, it is easy to see why creation science or intelligent design doesn't have a chance. Any attempt to present it in a state-funded classroom as a legitimate alternative to evolution will be blocked by the state's unwillingness (given the establishment clause) to give its stamp of approval to a religious position. Any attempt to remove the label "religious" and replace it with "scientific" will be resisted by the arbiters of what science is, who have already made up their collective mind in advance. And any attempt to establish the truth of intelligent design by the usual academic routes of argument and experiment will not get off the ground because the academy, like the liberal state of which it is a mirror and an extension, defines itself by its difference from religion. (In 1915, the American Association of University Professors denied the name "university" to religiously funded and sponsored institutions because "genuine boldness and thoroughness of inquiry" were incompatible with the "prescribed inculcation" of a set of beliefs.) Try as it might, creation science or, if you prefer, intelligent design, has not succeeded in freeing itself from its origin in religious dogma, and the various efforts to break free are regarded as suspect and illegitimate by the very disciplinary authorities it hopes to persuade. (I trust it is clear that in describing the mechanisms by which creationist arguments are excluded from serious academic discussions, I am not making a case either for or against their inclusion.)

For some time now ID proponents have been trying to get their arguments in through the back door by abstracting away from their specific claims and repackaging their cause in the language of open inquiry: if establishment authorities say that our ideas don't hold up, why not let the chips fall where they may in the course of free and uninhibited debate; let's not avoid the controversy, let's *teach* the controversy (a slogan they borrow from Gerald Graff). The response on the part of the establishment is predictable: there *is* no controversy (which means that this inquiry is not open), and by pretending that there is one you are just trying to create an opening for your entirely specious arguments (as Satan did when he said to Eve, "Indeed?"). As usual Judge Jones agreed with the establishment: "ID's backers have sought to avoid the scientific scrutiny which we have now determined that it cannot withstand by advocating that the *controversy*, but not ID itself, should be taught in science classes. This tactic is at best disingenuous and at worst a canard." With this avenue blocked, the ID proponents have no way to get in. Although the academy is the place for argument and arguments for intelligent design abound, you're not going to find them in the classroom or in peer-reviewed essays except as the rejected-in-advance object of a condescending description.

This does not mean that there is no hope. The academy is not a static place and the roster of acceptable and unacceptable arguments is not fixed. Andrew Abbott calculates that "twenty years is about the length of time it takes a group of academics to storm the ramparts, take the citadel, and settle down to the fruits of victory" (*Chaos of Disciplines*). During the process, the two groups—the stormers of the citadel and its defenders— will have different lists of acceptable and unacceptable arguments. When the process is over (at least for a while), one list will be the discipline's official one, until, and inevitably, the process starts all over again. Fluctuation in the content of the distinction between acceptable and unacceptable arguments is less significant in the long run than the fact that the distinction, in some form, is always in place. Academics always know what they can say and what they cannot say, and that knowledge remains a hallmark of their membership in the enterprise even when it is being debated. Creationism may yet have its day in the academy, but I don't see it coming soon.

Do Academic Arguments Matter?

The question of what academics can and cannot say is distinct from the question of what happens when they say it. What are the effects of academic arguments? While the academy and the law are alike in the narrowness of the range of arguments they allow to be made, they differ in the consequences that follow once an argument has succeeded in the discipline. A successful academic argument has as its fruit the judgment that one scholar is right and another wrong about a disputed matter. A successful legal argument has as *its* fruit the dispersion of rewards and penalties not only to those who are party to the instant case, but to those down the line (friends, relatives, associates) who will be impacted by the decision. The law professor Robert Cover famously began an essay by declaring, "Legal Interpretation takes place in a field of pain and death" ("Violence and the Word," *Yale Law Journal*, 1986). By that he meant that while legal argument may appear to be dispassionate and impartial—made without respect to persons—real, live persons are affected by them in real and sometimes awful ways: "When [legal] interpreters have finished their work, they frequently leave behind victims whose lives have been torn apart by . . . organized, social practices of violence." To be sure, the loser in an academic argument may suffer a diminution of his or her reputation, may fail to be offered a plum job, may not be elected president of the discipline's association, but this is a far cry from losing your property or losing your money or losing custody of your child or losing your freedom or losing your life. Although consequences follow from being vanquished in either field of argument, the consequences of defeat in the one seem more substantial than the consequences of defeat in the other. Indeed, it may not be too much to say that it is a feature of academic warfare that its outcomes are *supposed* to be inconsequential in the larger order of things.

Sometimes this is obvious, as it was when an academic brouhaha broke out in the pages of the *Times Literary Supplement* many years ago. In 1934, a dispute arose over the subject of an infinitive in lines 45–46 of John Milton's "L'Allegro": "Then to come in spite of sorrow / And at my window bid good morrow." The question at issue was who or what comes to the window, and the scholars who weighed in (some of the leading lights in seventeenth-century literary criticism) offered as the right answer nearly every noun or name in the previous ten lines. Over the weeks, the exchanges grew more heated, and when one participant declared that it is "vain to argue such questions" (because they cannot be conclusively resolved), another thundered that it is a matter of "Milton's poetic honor" that he not be read in a way that makes him "talk nonsense." The controversy ends not with a bang but a whimper when the editors announce, "We cannot continue this correspondence." Of course, they could have continued it forever and made all the participants happy (although readers less interested in Milton's poetic honor would have been less happy). It was what they lived for—debating the ever finer points of a matter in which perhaps five hundred people in the entire world were interested.

But wouldn't it be different with a matter less esoteric than the subject of an infinitive in one of Milton's minor poems? If the topic of discussion were the alternative strategies for dealing with Iran or the reality of global warming or the merits and demerits of "broken-windows" policing or the tactics of the Tea Party, wouldn't the arguments being made by academics either in the classroom or in a scholarly essay be more consequential than any argument about the syntax of a seventeenth-century poem?

Actually, no. The structure and effect of the discussion would be exactly the same as long as it was an academic discussion and not something else. You can—and, if you're a classroom teacher, should—study the rise of the Tea Party, its strategies, its place on the ideological map, its political prospects, without at any point rendering an up or down judgment on its philosophy or agenda. You can turn an analytical lens on the broken-windows theory of community policing and examine crime statistics before and after it was introduced in a municipality and still be miles from announcing that you would support or reject it were you a member of a city council. The consequences of there being a Tea Party are considerable and the consequences of community policing are arguably greater, but there are *no* consequences to the academic study of either, except for the consequence in a classroom of a clearer view of the subject or the consequence for a career of having written a seminal article. Again, these are not small consequences in the internal world of the academy, but they do not spill over into the larger world where they provoke men, women, and armies to action.

To be sure, national and even global consequences may follow if what you have said in class or written in a scholarly essay is picked up and cited by someone who is in a position to advance an agenda. But such consequences are contingent; they are not built into the academic enterprise and they may or may not occur. What can always occur, if you work hard enough, is that you and your students end the semester with a deeper understanding of an issue, an event, a text, an idea, a physical phenomenon, and that should be more than enough, although it is not for many instructors. Academic arguments don't move mountains, they move minds (which may down the road move mountains, but again that is a contingent outcome), and thus in a way they are weightless, that is, without weight in the give and take of political strife unless they are appropriated for political purposes. But their weightlessness is their glory, and that is why they are different from domestic arguments, political arguments, and legal arguments. Like virtue, the making of them is their own reward. Other rewards are left to time and heaven.

CHAPTER 6

WHY WE CAN'T GET ALONG

◆――――◆

Everything Is an Argument

IN THE CHAPTERS before this last one I have been assuming—without flagging or defending the assumption—that argument is the practice of offering propositions about a contested matter and responding to competing propositions by citing evidence and giving reasons. Argument involves the exchanging of words. But, as we have always known, arguments come in nonverbal forms—in gestures, colors, musical refrains, and, above all, in images. Argument, in short, is embodied; it doesn't take place in just the head but involves almost everything that comes before our eyes. What is now called "visual rhetoric" has been around at least since the elaborate description of Achilles' shield in Homer's *Iliad*, book 18, and arguably since the Egyptian hieroglyphics.

But is visual rhetoric argumentative in the appropriate sense? Do images make assertions in a way that renders them "a legitimate tool of rational persuasion," as opposed to emotional persuasion, which certainly occurs but is usually thought to be inferior and suspect? The answer has often been no, but J. Anthony Blair makes a good case for saying yes when he analyzes a pre–World War II cartoon by David Low depicting "an evidently complacent Englishman . . . reading a newspaper, sitting directly underneath a jumble of precariously balanced boulders" ("The Rhetoric of Visual Arguments," *Defining Visual Rhetorics*, 2004).

The boulder at the bottom is marked "Czecho" and the caption reads, "What's Czechoslovakia to me, anyway?" The propositional content of the cartoon, Blair explains, is "that to regard the fate of Czechoslovakia as having no consequences is mistaken," and the reasoning supporting the proposition is that if Czechoslovakia were to fall to Germany, the other precariously placed boulders—labelled "Rumania," "Poland," "French Alliances," and "Anglo-French Security"—would fall down too. (How's that for political prophecy?) Blair concludes that "to the objection that propositions cannot be expressed visually the reply is that because it has been done in Low's cartoon, it is possible" (48).

Blair could also have found support in the ancient traditions of emblem books, religious iconography, bestiaries, heraldry, illustrated fables, and other literary/cultural forms that present moralized images, images with propositional content. The figure Rhetorica from the "Tarot Cards of Mantegna" (1467) is a nice example because it makes a point about visual rhetoric visually. It shows an imposing female figure, standing with an upraised sword at a ninety-degree angle to her outstretched arm; although her feet are bare, her clothing is rich and elaborately draped; she wears a long, flowing garment adorned by a jeweled breastplate; on top of the garment, secured just below the collarbone, is a purple cape, the hem of which she holds with her left hand; on her head sits a helmet topped with a crown; on either side of her two putti, also barefooted, blow trumpets, one pointing up, the other down.

The argument being made by this image is as easy to read as the argument being made by Low's cartoon: "You might have thought that rhetoric is the art of filigree and mere decoration, a weak feminine sister of forceful, manly verbal argument, but in fact the sword of rhetoric is mightier than even the military sword, for it can bring men low or raise them high simply by blowing either the trumpet of blame or the trumpet of praise; that is why the figure of Rhetorica is clothed in purple, the color worn by priests, cardinals, princes, kings, magistrates, and warriors, all bearers of a male authority that is superseded by Queen Rhetoric, resplendent in her crown." All that and more (I didn't get to the breastplate and helmet and bare feet) is conveyed at a glance by the image, which exemplifies the truth it preaches: arguments made visually have "more force and immediacy than verbal communication allows" (Blair, 53).

Blair doesn't want to make the concept of visual rhetoric so broad that it includes any image at all. In order to count as an argument, an image must, he insists, "render vivid and immediate . . . a reason or set of reasons offered for modifying a belief, an attitude or one's conduct" (50). That standard, he tells us, is not met by many familiar, even iconic, images, like the image of the Marlboro Man: "A billboard with a picture of a cowboy with a tattoo on a horse smoking a cigarette. Visual influence? Absolutely. Visual argument? None" (58).

Wrong. It's an argument about image and self-esteem. The proposition is that you should smoke Marlboro cigarettes rather than smoke another brand or not smoke at all; the reasoning is that if you do, you will be that much closer to being lean, rugged, independent, self-reliant, self-branding, mobile, and adventurous. The argument can be criticized for being shallow and meretricious because it equates well-being with surface characteristics, but that is the argument built into almost all advertising: X is a good or desirable thing to have or be; purchasing our product is the way to achieve X (happiness, beauty, popularity, influence, respect, love, wealth); therefore you should purchase our product. The middle term is specious—you can't purchase the real thing, only a simulacrum—but it works.

The Marlboro Man ad is literally a fashion statement, with the emphasis on "statement": it proclaims values and tells you how to live. Fashion is never merely the announcement that this cut or accessory or length is now in and others are out of fashion; the new wrinkle, whatever it is, sends a message about identity, status, political affiliation, and a thousand other things. In her brilliant study *Seeing Through Clothes* (1978), Anne Hollander provides example after example of the complex, propositional messages sent by clothing. From the very beginning, she observes, there was a connection "between draped cloth and lofty concepts," and although there is "no evidence that wearing full, draped clothing ever made anyone nobler . . . the association of the idea of drapery with the idea of a better and more beautiful life flourished" (2–3).

Other associations of ideas with clothing include the dandy's wearing of fitted black clothes to indicate an artistic temperament and an alienation from society, even as he displayed to society an apparent negligence that required "exacting hours before the mirror" (229). At the other extreme are those who "dress down" in an effort to declare an admirable indifference to what they wear. Hollander notes that in every age, some of the high and the mighty who can easily afford extravagance nevertheless embrace "the notion that unassuming costume is the sign of more serious temperament or more refined aesthetic taste," a taste that is not a slave to fashion (257–58). But as she points out, the trouble with this anti-fashion strategy is that others will soon imitate it and it will become the "fashionable thing" it tries to avoid. "Those who create anti-fashion are themselves products of the coercion they wish to ignore" (365).

It is never possible, Hollander says, to just "wear anything" and think by your studied carelessness to avoid making a statement, although the statement you make will vary over time as colors and styles (short skirt, low skirt, cinched waist, full waist, belt, no belt, hat, no hat, baggy pants, fitted pants, high neckline, plunging neckline) take on ever new significance in the turns of the history of fashion. In that history, fully elaborated by Hollander, black more than any other color is the medium of multiple messages, depending on which of the "two aspects of black clothing—the conventionally sober, self-denying black and the dramatic, isolating, and distinguished black" is in vogue (377); but the one thing black will never be is just black; an argument is always being made. After all, you've got to wear something—if not black, white, purple, or red; if not cotton, linen, denim, or silk—and even if you were to wear nothing and go naked you would still be sending out messages and declaring a position; for clothes or their absence cannot help but "suggest, persuade, connote, insinuate, or indeed lie" (355) (when your clothes say one thing but your heart means another).

What is true of clothing is true also of furniture, restaurant interiors, hairstyles, automobiles, boats, apartments, city-street grids, landscape gardening, baseball stadiums, airplanes, storefronts, book jackets, television sets, smart phones: each is characterized by an intentional arrangement of components, by choices of size, shape, material, dimension, finish; in each instance those arrangements and choices say something, often in contrast or opposition to what has been said previously (modernist architecture celebrates the unity of form and function; unity is what postmodern architecture mocks); and as customers or consumers or viewers we affirm or reject the messages that emanate from everything we see. The world, at least the world of man-made artifacts, is just one argument after another, a point made crisply by Andrea Lunsford and John Ruszkiewicz: "all language, including the language of visual images, is persuasive, pointing in a direction and asking for a response" (*Everything's an Argument*, 1998).

A Modern Version of the Desire
to Escape Argument

Enlarging the scope of argument to include images, cloth-ing, jewelry, and everything else runs the risk of feeding into the distrust of argument—really the distrust of language—harbored by those who yearn for the unvarnished truth and are therefore wary of any intermediary layer—be it verbal or material—placed between them and the possibility of what Jürgen Habermas calls "undistorted communication." Undistorted communication is communication from which the wrong motives—instrumental, strategic—are excluded so that only a single motive, "that of the cooperative search for truth," is allowed (*Legitimation Crisis*, 1975). This means that participants refrain from making arguments that reflect their own interests and resolve instead (just how this resolve is to be executed is the problem) to make arguments that flow from and toward a common interest in establishing a universal truth assented to by everyone. Those who make and receive such arguments will be speaking the same language because they will have harnessed themselves to the same impersonal discourse: "all participants stick to the reference point of . . . achieving a mutual understanding in which the same utter-ances are assigned the same meaning."

It's a promise and an agenda we have met before: language use will be put on the right path by filtering out everything that acknowledges interest and difference, that is, the fact that we are not all the same. Orwell thinks that communi-cation can be purified by being careful about the individual words you use. Habermas thinks that communication can be purified by being careful about what kinds of arguments you make. It is the lesson of the marriage manuals universalized. The difference is that in the manuals the disavowing of interest is performed (in a rigidly constrained discourse context) with the hope of securing a harmony between just two persons; the harmony sought is local and is, at least occasionally, achievable. The harmony sought by Habermas is universal.

It seems like an attractive program until you ask questions such as: How do you know when participants have set aside pragmatic and strategic considerations and moved to the higher state of being disinterested in the strongest sense of that word? How do you know when one of the participants in the ideal speech situation is only pretending to have broken with the purposes that have hitherto motivated him and is holding one of them up his sleeve on the reasoning that "after all, I'm right, and it would be unwise to surrender everything I believe for the vague promise of some intersubjective nirvana"?

The answer to these questions is that you can't know, or, rather, you can't know unless you can identify and occupy some independent, nonangled perspective—a contradiction in terms—from which judgments on sincerity and purity of motive can be securely and noncontroversially made. But if such a perspective were available, if good and bad arguments—arguments aimed at a consensual understanding versus arguments aimed at prevailing—were self-identifying, the discursive realm would *already* be the place cleansed of preference and bias to which discourse ethics is supposed to bring us. If we could get to that place by an act of will, by first cataloging and then renouncing the presupposed norms that produce distortion, there would be no need for the elaborate machinery and severe cautions that make up Habermas's project. When he directs us to "start with concrete speech acts embedded in specific contexts and then disregard all aspects those utterances owe to their pragmatic functions" (the functions they perform in ordinary angled speech), I hear "disregard" as an imperative waiting for a technology, for a set of directions that never arrives. How do you do it?

Habermas's surprising answer to this question is that we are already doing it because every time we open our mouths to say something we have committed ourselves to validating what we say by universal norms. From the beginning we're already partway there. All we have to do is grasp that part of our utterance that is not tied to a limited, instrumental aim and run with it. "[A]nyone acting communicatively must, in performing any speech action, raise universal validity claims and suppose they can be vindicated" (*Communication and the Evolution of Society*, 1979). We may be saying things like "here is what we must do" or "I think you are flat wrong," but at bottom what we're really saying is "let's work toward intersubjective praxis." It may seem that each of us is interested in the triumph of a particular point of view, but in fact our true interest, even when our statements take an agonistic form, is to join with others in securing a general consensus.

I see no reason to believe this to be so. When I try to

persuade you to my point of view, my intentions are entirely strategic. I want to get you on my side and there is no larger communicative goal (like universal understanding) to which my contextually situated effort aspires (behind my back as it were). Habermas appears to think that we are all philosophers operating within philosophical (not forensic) ambitions even when we say, "I think the policy you recommend is wrong" or "I think we should bomb Iran now." If we *were* all philosophers, if philosophy were built into our everyday speech acts rather than being a very specialized discourse of interest to only a few people, it would make sense to say that the goal of our every utterance was its transcendence. But saying we are all philosophers doesn't make it so. And unless we are all philosophers, engaged always in the raising of universal validity claims, the realm of instrumental purposes is the realm we will always live in.

Escaping that realm is not an option—there's no way out—and asserting that we have already escaped it by virtue of some genetically wired orientation to universality undercuts both the urgency and the point of Habermas's enterprise. Whether you agree or disagree with Habermas's account of language as a universalizing engine, the project has nowhere to go. If he is right about the intersubjective hopes built into ordinary discourse, his utopian conversational ideal has already been realized, so what's the fuss all about? If he is wrong and conversation is irremediably situated and local, his program of purifying discourse is a nonstarter (just as Orwell's was) because there is no place for the would-be purifier to stand; the entire field is saturated with interest.

How Both Liberalism and Religion Look
Forward to the End of Argument

The failure of Habermas's project is an instance of the general failure of liberal rationalism, the project of establishing a common ground rooted not in obedience to a deity or to an overarching moral order, but in a thin proceduralism. Liberalism—and by that word I mean the Enlightenment philosophical program inaugurated by Kant, not a position on the political continuum—seeks to avoid the conflicts that arise when substantive agendas fight it out in the public square by substituting procedural norms for the interest-laden norms that produce social and political division. (The idea is to fashion laws that match, insofar as possible, the minimal content of the rule mandating that we all drive on the same side of the road; who could argue with that?)

The first step in the liberal program is to dethrone God or any pregiven morality as the source of meaning, because there is no version of God or morality to which all members of the citizenry assent. The next step is to come up with a replacement for what has been dethroned, to come up with a mechanism that provides the same generality of meaning that was provided (at least for believers) by revealed Truth. The value liberalism substitutes for obedience to a higher authority is the value of choice as it is exercised by a free and autonomous individual. But freedom, autonomy, and choice are problematic values if the goal is to fashion a polity where conflict has given way to agreement and harmony, at least with respect to basic foundational matters. Give freedom of choice full sway and it will produce the very divisiveness from which liberalism promises to rescue us. How can the freely choosing individual be constrained in a way that avoids a Hobbesian war of all against all, now that suprarational constraints like God and moral absolutes have been repudiated?

The answer given in the liberal tradition will be familiar to readers of this book: forge a language devoid of substantive hostages, a language of such generality and metaphysical emptiness that to speak it is to commit oneself to almost nothing. The thinness of its terms and definitions ensures that it will be intelligible and acceptable to anyone, no matter what he or she happened to believe, or not believe, about God or the shape of moral truth. If such a language (akin to the neutral observation language Kuhn declares unavailable) could be devised and adherence to it were required of everyone who entered the public sphere, the decisions reached in the political process would be truly communal because they would depend not on variable and contested beliefs, but on matters of social fact encoded in a language common to all.

Given this linguistic/ethical program, it is easy to see why public discourse in the liberal state cannot accommodate religion and religious arguments. Religion does not consider itself bound by the norms of empirical validation; instead it is answerable only to the norms of faith, norms that refuse to be judged by any standard but their own, norms that are affirmed and adhered to no matter what the world and its socially approved methodologies deliver as truth. When strong believers converse with one another, the vocabulary they deploy points to (but does not contain) realities that are powerfully present for them, yet inaccessible to those outside the fold. Therefore a public language that was doing its job of enabling rational consensus cannot contain religious terms and concepts. Liberalism's hope of a community of rational choosers is incompatible with religion.

That incompatibility becomes painfully obvious when religious commitments clash with the commitments encoded in secular law. In the summer of 2015, Kim Davis, an elected county clerk in Kentucky, declared herself unable to issue marriage licenses to same-sex couples because her religion restricted marriage to the union of a man and a woman. The national debate that erupted when a judge declared her in contempt and sent her to jail pitted those who insisted that she was obligated to follow the law she had sworn to execute against those who insisted that she was obligated to follow the higher law of her faith. Neither side gave an inch, and in innumerable op-eds, sermons, and radio talk-show conversations, a familiar point-counterpoint played itself out in predictable ways.

One side, the side of faith, said that religion speaks to our highest aspirations and no one should be asked to abandon those aspirations just because a merely secular law, interpreted strictly and without due concern for the claims of conscience, requires it. The other side, the classically liberal side, argued that those aspirations are attached to a faith not shared by everyone—they are not *public* aspirations—and it is wrong to allow one person, especially a person in office, to hold herself above a law that has been established democratically and applies to all citizens; Kim Davis is free to think and believe anything she likes, but she is not free to impose her beliefs on others who are denied their rights by her actions. The response came back saying that the state is denying *her* rights under the Free Exercise clause of the First Amendment by refusing to accommodate her strong and sincerely held religious convictions. But, declared the counterresponse, if we grant that accommodation to her, don't we have to grant accommodations to anyone who claims to be moved by some inner prompting, and won't we end up with a government not of laws but of men (and women), all lawgivers to themselves? And won't that mean the death of law and the destruction of civil order? And so it went, and so it goes to this very day. As Milton might have said, "And of their vain contest appeared no end."

And yet, although religion and liberalism are locked in an opposition for which there is no resolution, they are alike in one respect—their claim to be universal, albeit in different ways. Liberal universalism is to be achieved by subtraction, by removing or bracketing comprehensive moral dictates not everyone would recognize; religious universalism is inherent in the comprehensive claim of a religion to be bearing a truth everyone, including nonbelievers, should acknowledge. One kind of universalism says, "be an independent, rational chooser rather than someone chosen and scripted by deity or a pregiven morality"; the other says, "forgo your independence—you really don't have it anyway—and allow yourself to be absorbed into a structure not made by hands."

In the shared context of their quite different universalisms, liberalism and religion share something else: they are both suspicious of argument, the first because argument, if pursued beyond the level of the procedural, tends to unsettle a political order that depends on procedure and the avoidance of substance to hold it together (you can argue about little things, but not about big, metaphysical, things); the second because religion privileges obedience and conformity to the divine will and regards argument as a sign of distance from the peace that passeth understanding. It is no exaggeration to say that a desire for argument's death is built into the tradition that names the fruit of the forbidden tree in Genesis the apple of discord.

Before the Fall, the story goes, harmony and unity were the rule, but when pride—the desire to stand out among one's fellows—infected first Satan and then Adam and Eve, discord began its long tenure. Ever since, philosophy, theology, and ethics have been devising ways to reverse the Fall's effects and return us to an Edenic state in which peace and good will once again reign, and argument will be superfluous. Oh, if we could only stop bickering, if both individuals and states could only put aside their disagreements rooted in the base impulses of acquisitiveness and the will to power and learn to live together. In the words of Rodney King, can't we all just get along? Can't we damp down the noise, soft-pedal the acrimony, let go of the scorn, withdraw from judgment, find common ground, give one another a break?

Argument and the Unredeemed World

Deborah Tannen asks the same questions from a secular perspective in her aptly titled *The Argument Culture: Stopping America's War of Words* (1998). Tannen surveys the public scene and argues (an irony of which she is very much aware), "Our spirits are corroded by living in an atmosphere of unrelenting opposition—an argument culture" (3). She observes, "Our public interactions have become more and more like having an argument with a spouse," because when you're having that kind of argument, "your goal is not to listen and understand. Instead you use every tactic you can think of . . . in order to win" (4–5). The compulsion to win an argument mandates an oppositional stance and therefore "privileges extreme views and obscures complexity . . . and poisons our relations with one another," and that means, she contends, that "the argument culture is doing more damage than good" (25).

Tannen is particularly hard on the argument culture of the academy, where the need "to make others wrong" leads you, she says, "to search for the most foolish statement in a generally reasonable treatise, seize upon the weakest examples, ignore facts that support your opponent's views, and focus only on those that support yours" (269). The rules of the academic game as I described them earlier are the objects of Tannen's criticism here. Rather than reading with an open mind, students in the grip of the argument culture act out the lesson "that they must disprove others' arguments in order to be original" (269). Sometimes it seems, she muses, that the "maxim driving academic discourse" is "if you can't find anything bad to say, don't say anything" (269).

It is not surprising that Tannen's strictures have drawn a vigorous response from Gerald Graff, who invented the pedagogic strategy of "teaching the controversies." (It's his big idea.) Graff acknowledges that argumentation can take a bad turn and become little more than vituperation or "trash talk," but he insists on its "unavoidable centrality . . . to democratic societies and educational institutions," and he questions whether Tannen's preferred mode, dialogue, is really a distinct form and not a variant of the argumentative form she wants it to replace: "Tannen overstates the distinction between debate and dialogue, which form a continuum rather than an opposition"; for "conversation alternates between adversarial and consensual moments and often pauses as we reflect on which mode we're in" ("Two Cheers for the Argument Culture," *Hedgehog Review*, 2000). This moment of reflection, within and not apart from the argumentative field, is the closest thing there is to the "reflective moment" Habermas offers as the way to escape argument. But it affords no escape. Stepping back in a moment of reflection from the context of argument is an act performed within and shaped by that context. Consensual moments certainly occur, and when they do the edge of argument is softened as a stylistic matter, but it is still argument you are engaging in (consensus is a part of strategy, not an exit from it) and, indeed, you have no choice if you agree with Michael Billig (as Graff does) when he says that "argument is the root of thought" (*Arguing and Thinking:*

A Rhetorical Approach to Social Psychology, 1996). No argument means no assertion, no exploration of alternatives, no movement, no advance in knowledge, no building of community.

While Habermas and Tannen, in their very different ways, want to pull argument's sting and find a way out of it, Leon Wieseltier wants to do the reverse. He wants to fully and joyously engage in, not transcend, verbal conflict. He observes that more and more these days, "a shared understanding is preferred to a multiplicity of understandings, which is rejected as an epistemologically fallen condition" ("The Argumentative Jew," *Jewish Review of Books*, 2015). He refers to this preference as a "consensualist mentality" and the "cult of unanimity," and he opposes to it the tradition of the argumentative Jew, which, he says, "displays an almost erotic relationship to controversy." Controversy, the back-and-forth of argument, is what is left to us when the "God's-eye view" is unavailable, and Wieseltier is not one of those who believes (against all the lessons of history) that the earthly heaven of undistorted communication and unanimity of opinion is waiting for us at controversy's end.

Rather than envisioning a progressive enlarging of perspectives as Habermas does, Wieseltier celebrates the give-and-take of vigorous exchange, which if engaged in wholeheartedly creates a community of persons who continue to disagree: "The parties to a disagreement . . . belong to the group that wrestles together with the same perplexity, and they wrestle together for the sake of the larger community to which they all belong." "A quarrel," Wieseltier declares, "is evidence of coexistence." It is evidence that we are all in the same boat, trying to figure things out in the absence of clear direction from a deity, and offering to one another, sometimes with an aggressive edge, analyses and arguments we are obliged to answer. In this "model of quarrelsome unity"—unity as a function of, not an escape from, agon—we learn "to live with disagreement and not to think less of it because it cannot be miraculously consummated." Disagreement—argument—Wieseltier roundly declares, "is not only real, it is also an ideal—at least in the unredeemed world, the only world we know."

An unredeemed world is a world where final meanings of the kind that would stop conflict in its tracks are not available. The choice—and it really isn't one—is to live with that reality or search for ways to neutralize it or get around it, which are really ways of denying it. What is being denied by the various schemes and methods surveyed in these pages is the inescapably contextual and mediated nature of human experience. The famous verse in 1 Corinthians reads, "Now we see through a glass darkly, but then face to face" (13:12). The glass (or perspective or lens or mirror) through which we now see is the glass of human limitation. Situated as we are in the midst of—not to the side of—local perspectives, ever-challengeable assumptions, imperfect information, and ungrounded beliefs, "face to face" seeing will be ours only when the condition of mortality has been left behind, when we have been absorbed into the perfect wholeness of vision and understanding now (literally) beyond us, when the differences that now divide us are revealed—and "revealed" should be understood very strongly—to be inessential and ultimately unreal.

Every "projector" whose messianic promises we have encountered along the way tells us that the arrival of that happy day can be accelerated by some device or insight or magic key that at once identifies and removes the obstacles to perfect communication. Getting rid of ambiguities, metaphors, figures of speech, and fictions, using only simple words that point directly to things (somehow self-identifying), hewing closely to facts (somehow self-identifying), taking care to put forward only impersonal arguments (also somehow self-identifying), devising a language from which substance has been exiled—these, supposedly, are the levers by which we can hoist ourselves to the heaven of static-free, perfectly transparent conversation while remaining earth-bound.

The latest vaunted vehicle of "paradise here and now" is the Internet, whose most fervent apostles predict that because of it war, inequality, confusion, want, and poverty will disappear and be replaced by a perfect democracy in which every voice is equally heard and equally valued and none can claim precedence. These new prophets (sounding very much like the old prophets) believe, Evgeny Morozov explains, that factions, ideological disagreements, and deep conflict "are simply the unfortunate result of an imperfect communication infrastructure" (*To Save Everything, Click Here: The Folly of Technological Solutionism*, 2013). The "fundamental assumption," Morozov adds, is that "disagreements occur not because people are bound to differ, but because they are misinformed." They are misinformed because what they hear and receive is filtered through institutions, political parties, biased media, and other vehicles of interest and distortion. "Solutionists" believe we can bypass those vehicles and free ourselves from their baneful influence by engaging directly with information via "open networks"—networks that are uncensored, without gatekeepers and therefore antiauthoritarian. We will thus become capable of seeing the undistorted truth, and our decisions about what to do and whom to elect (if elections are still necessary) will be instantaneous and epistemologically clean. Don't go to meetings or contribute to candidates or hew to a party line; just look, face-to-face, and click.

In this techno-utopia, "organized political parties won't be needed" because people will "organize ad hoc, rather than get stuck in some rigid group" (Esther Dyson, quoted in "The Merry Pranksters Go to Washington," *Wired*, 1994). The result will be the elimination of politics altogether, for we will be able to, according to Morozov, "replace politicians and politics with technocrats." Formerly political questions can be decided scientifically through algorithms, so there will be "no need to waste time discussing their merits and perpetuating all the messiness of the political process." All that will be left to what we used to call politics will be "fixing potholes and dealing with stray dogs."

So once again, and for the umpteenth time, we see the desire to eliminate difference and the confidence that we can do so by either devising a neutral observation language or, in this brave new Internet world, by the frictionless exchanging of information that has been cleansed of ideological encrustations. Such information, unsponsored and uninflected by bias and strategic motives, speaks for itself to clear-eyed observers who needn't engage in any adversarial argumentative battles because everyone sees and registers the same unfiltered thing. This is what Beth Noveck, described by Morozov as an "open government advocate," celebrates as the "public exchange of reason"; not an exchange in which your reasons and my reasons might clash, but the public exchange of reasons that, because they issue from a base of commonly shared, interpretation-free data, have the capacity to create community all by themselves without the intervening and distorting screen of argument. "People," Noveck enthuses, "can 'speak' through shared maps and diagrams" without having to talk, without having to use words. It's *Gulliver's Travels* all over again, offered this time not as satire, but as salvation. Instead of things taken out of a backpack, we will have raw data untainted by the corruption of subjectivity and therefore capable of generating meaning and agreement simply by virtue of getting bigger and bigger. Language, always vulnerable to manipulation, kills, but big data saveth. (Actually, you could pile up data until it stood higher than ten Empire State Buildings and it wouldn't tell you anything.)

As I said earlier, this is a dream that dies hard. In fact it will never die, and it will survive every effort to puncture its balloon, including mine. I can say till the end of time what I have said over and over in these pages—that the wish to escape argument is really the wish to escape language, which is really the wish to escape politics, and is finally the wish to escape mortality—and it won't matter a whit. For one effect of inhabiting the condition of difference—the condition of being partial, the condition of not being in direct touch with the final unity and full meaning of the universe—is that we long to transcend it; and it is that longing, forever disappointed, that keeps us going.

ACKNOWLEDGMENTS

◆———————◆

ONCE AGAIN Julia Cheiffetz of HarperCollins didn't let me rest until I produced a book that someone might actually want to read.

Sean Newcott kept track of all the changes and variants, and put up with the author's computer illiteracy.

Joanna Pinsker thought of ways to spread the news.

I benefitted greatly from the friendly but exacting readings provided by Larry Alexander, Peter Goodrich, Jerry Graff, Arthur Jacobson, Peter Lushing, Steve Mailloux, David McGowan, Michael Robertson, Maimon Schwarzschild, Jane Tompkins, and Richard Weisberg.

Melissa Flashman, as always, negotiated, ran interference, and generally took care of me.

Thank you all.

ABOUT THE AUTHOR

◆———————◆

STANLEY FISH IS the visiting Floersheimer Distinguished Professor of Law at Cardozo Law School in
New York City and the Davidson-Kahn Distinguished
University Professor and a professor of law at Florida
International University. He has previously taught at
the University of California at Berkeley, Johns Hop-
kins University, Duke University, and the University
of Illinois at Chicago, where he was dean of the College of Liberal Arts and Sciences. He has received many
honors and awards, including being named the Chica-
goan of the Year for Culture. He resides in Andes, New
York; New York City; and Highland Beach, Florida,
with his wife, Jane Tompkins.

ALSO BY STANLEY FISH

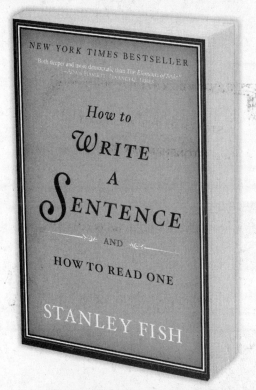

HOW TO WRITE A SENTENCE
And How to Read One
Available in Paperback and Ebook

"Both deeper and more democratic than *The Elements of Style*."
— Adam Haslett, *Financial Times*

"A guided tour through some of the most beautiful, arresting sentences
in the English language."
— *Slate*

In this entertaining and erudite *New York Times* bestseller, beloved professor Stanley Fish offers both sentence craft and sentence pleasure. Drawing on a wide range of great writers, from Philip Roth to Antonin Scalia to Jane Austen, *How to Write a Sentence* is much more than a writing manual—it is a spirited love letter to the written word, and a key to understanding how great writing works.

Available Wherever Books Are Sold